MW01712864

Canadian Biography Series

ALEX COLVILLE: THE OBSERVER OBSERVED

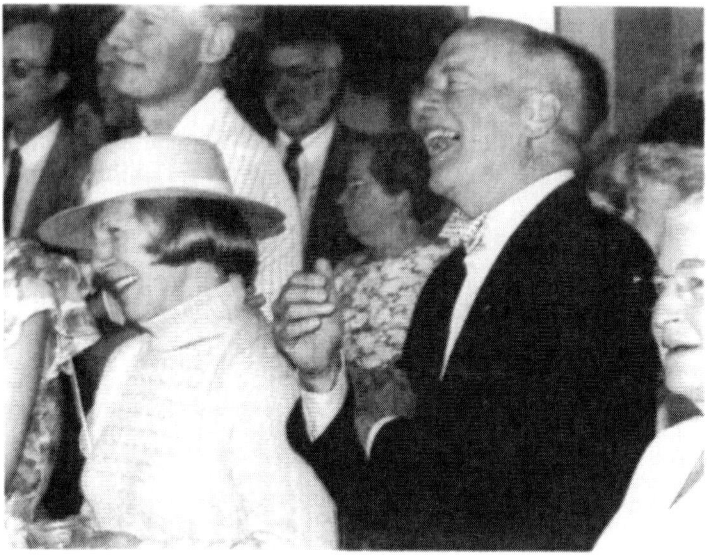

Alex and Rhoda Colville at a reception for Dr. and Mrs. James Perkin, Acadia University, June 1993.

Alex Colville

THE OBSERVER OBSERVED

Mark A. Cheetham

ECW PRESS

CANADIAN CATALOGUING IN PUBLICATION DATA

Cheetham, Mark A. (Mark Arthur), 1954–
Alex Colville : the observer observed

Includes bibliographical references.
ISBN 1-55022-206-6

1. Colville, Alex, 1920– . 2. Painters – Canada – Biography. I. Title.

ND249.C58C54 1994 759.11 C94-930008-X

This book has been published with the assistance of the Ministry of Culture, Recreation and Tourism of the Province of Ontario, through funds provided by the Ontario Publishing Centre, and with the assistance of grants from the Department of Communications, The Canada Council, the Ontario Arts Council, and the Government of Canada through the Canadian Studies and Special Projects Directorate of the Department of the Secretary of State of Canada.

Design and imaging by ECW Type & Art, Oakville, Ontario.

Published by ECW PRESS,
1980 Queen Street East,
Toronto, Ontario M4L 1J2.

ACKNOWLEDGEMENTS

Writing a biography has made me reconsider the status of both artist and author today. Although both may consider themselves independent as they work, they rely not only on an extensive array of material for the inception and realization of their projects, but also on emotional and intellectual support. In analysing such enabling connections in Alex Colville's life, I have become keenly aware of, and grateful for, the people and institutions that have supported my own writing.

For crucial research funding, I wish to acknowledge the Social Sciences and Humanities Research Council of Canada and a Vice-President Research Special Competition Grant from the University of Western Ontario. Permission to quote from the programs *The Sweetest Spring* (1990) and *Diary of Alex Colville* (1965) was granted by the Canadian Broadcasting Corporation. I am grateful to the excellent staff at the Edward P. Taylor Research Library, Art Gallery of Ontario, for their help and permission to quote from documents in the Helen J. Dow Fonds. For timely assistance with photographs, thanks go to Laura Brandon at the Canadian War Museum and Marilyn Burnett at the Drabinsky Gallery.

Anyone writing about Colville is indebted to the pioneering work of David Burnett, on whose 1983 book *Colville* I rely considerably. For sharing their thoughts about Colville, I wish to thank David and Marilyn Burnett, Mira Godard, and Roly Fenwick. For proofreading, my thanks to Avril Flanigan.

Alex and Rhoda Colville were exceedingly gracious hosts when I was doing research in Wolfville. I have greatly appreciated Alex Colville's patience with my many questions, his precise answers, and his willingness to aid my work. His interest in the biography has — quite remarkably — remained at arm's length. True to his singular integrity and professionalism, he has been closely involved, but he has never interfered with my responsibility to interpret his life and work freely.

As always, my greatest debt is to Elizabeth Harvey for her extraordinary insight and enthusiasm, and to our son Nicholas for his good humour about serious topics. Viewing a new photographic reproduction of Colville's famous 1980 painting *Seven Crows*, the three-year-old art critic put everything in perspective by exclaiming, "Look, pterodactyls!"

PHOTOGRAPHS: Cover photo, 1991, is used by permission of The Drabinsky Gallery; frontispiece illustration, 1993, is used by permission of Alex Colville; illustration 2, 1968, is used by permission of Capital Press Ltd., Ottawa; illustration 3 is used by permission of The Drabinsky Gallery; illustration 4 is used by permission of the Art Gallery of Ontario; illustration 5, James Chambers, is used by permission of the Art Gallery of Ontario; illustration 6, 1943, is used by permission of Alex Colville; illustration 7, © 1993, is used by permission of the Canadian War Museum; illustration 8 is used by permission of The Drabinsky Gallery; illustration 9, 1928, is used by permission of Alex Colville; illustration 10, 1968, is used by permission of Alex Colville; illustration 11, c. 1955, is used by permission of Alex Colville; illustration 12 is used by permission of The Drabinsky Gallery; illustration 13, 1984, is used by permission of Alex Colville; illustration 14 is used by permission of the New Brunswick Museum; illustration 15 is used by permission of the Lavalin Collection, Musée d'art contemporain de Montréal; illustration 16, c. 1976, is used by permission of Henry Kahanek; illustration 17 is used by permission of the Art Gallery of Ontario; illustration 18, © 1977 Guido Mangold, is used by permission of Alex Colville; illustration 19 is used by permission of The Drabinsky Gallery; illustration 20, 1965, is used by permission of Alex Colville.

A NOTE ON THE TEXT

Because of the frequency of citation, page numbers are given in references to David Burnett, *Colville.*

For my Mother and Father

TABLE OF CONTENTS

LIST OF ILLUSTRATIONS

Alex Colville

THE OBSERVER OBSERVED

INTRODUCTION

Alex Colville is not always the man that we expect him to be. At seventy-three, he is a senior diplomat for the visual arts in Canada and probably this country's best-known living artist. Aware of his stature and its responsibilities, Colville is fittingly warm, courtly, and self-effacing in his many public roles. He is proud of his conservative nature and values. Yet when asked during an interview on *Stereo Morning* about his favourite musician, he says "k.d. lang!" Bach or Mozart would be more consistent with his interest in past art and precise composition. Colville has a penchant for fast cars and first-class hotels — leading Mira Godard, who knows him well, to say in an interview on 14 October 1992 that he is materially "acquisitive" — yet he lives a simple, rigorously ordered life in Wolfville, Nova Scotia, far from the fast lanes of Canadian culture and society.

Colville plays a part in Canadian society that goes beyond his position as a celebrated artist. He is a public figure. But there is no doubt that he has gained this position through his art, and that art remains the centre of his life. The phrase "life imitates art" helps us to understand what drives Colville. The force of this cliché turns on our recognition of its paradoxical nature. We are supposed to take it as normal that an artist's life comes logically and causally before his or her art and largely determines its content and shape. Common sense, it seems, dictates that "art imitates life," that art is controlled by the artist and represents his or her life. Biographers depend on this assumption: the more we know about the artist's life, the better we can understand the art. But when we come to Colville, the paradoxical notion that life imitates art becomes quite literally true: increasingly his life resembles one of his carefully planned and meticulously executed paintings.[1] Colville agrees with this characterization, pointing out in a personal interview that it has been accurate for some time: "I can remember being at some sort of conference, this is probably thirty years ago; I was sitting at a table drinking a glass of white wine, and Evan Turner [then Director of the Montreal Museum of Fine Arts] came by and said to me, 'You are just like your painting,' and of course it's true." So harmoniously intermingled are Colville's life and work that we learn more about him if we view his life as one of his paintings — rather than trying to separate art and life, as traditional biographies of other artists often do.

SELF-FASHIONING

If we resist the temptation to divide Colville's life and art, we see that he typically constructs his existence as carefully as his paintings and silk-screen prints. Speaking to students and faculty at the University of Guelph in 1988, Colville stressed the importance of art history to an artist's work and the essentially fictive nature of both artwork and artist. Margaret Boyd quotes him as saying, "an artist constructs a world in each work. It is a constructive, in some sense carpented and imagined [process], and in a certain sense an unreal world. When a person looks at it, the receiving of it, involves yet another construction."

The rigorous self-fashioning characteristic of Colville's life in art — with the resulting identification of life and art — is typical of many creative individuals. The psychologist Elisabeth Young-Bruel claims that "creative people have a particular kind of wish — a wish for self-ordering, self-organization — which is expressed, sometimes fulfilled, in all facets of their lives and work." If Colville harbours such a wish, and I think that he does, then it has certainly been fulfilled. In fact, the remarkable integration of Colville's life and work lead me to emphasize their habitual confluence. David Burnett — Colville's foremost chronicler and interpreter — writes that "It is a mark of special creative talent when, in reviewing the career of an artist, it is wrong to separate the work he has produced from the life he has led" (199). Colville himself affirms this view in a letter dated 15 January 1992: "I am inclined to think that divisions between 'the life' and 'the work' are false, at least in my case — I have tried to work at both." My primary goal is to detail *how* Colville's type of creativity has integrated his art and life, and what the results have been. Thus, in addition to giving biographical information, I will analyse his artistic products and comment on the degree to which they map his concerns, the ways in which they *are* his life.

Colville is a passionate and dedicated man, but his brand of creativity stands in sharp contrast to what has become the norm of artistic commitment: the creation of art through suffering and self-privation, best embodied in the Western tradition by the romanticized vision of Vincent van Gogh (1853–90). Colville creates art because his life is as ordered — even as comfortable — as his art aims to be, not because he wants to express life's profundities through his pain. He conserves his energy for his art, working at a measured pace, completing three works each year on average. He is a shrewd and effective manager of his resources. In contrast, van Gogh turned to art only in the final years of his short life. He expended his energy without thought and made art in spite of day-to-day hardship. Colville offers an alternative form of artistic production. Yet even in this he can surprise us: at the end of World War II, for example, Colville made the effort to visit van Gogh's descendants in the Netherlands to see some of Vincent's work, an intriguing pilgrimage for one so notoriously uninterested in the personalities of other artists. "I've always liked his work," Colville says in the interview, adding that his own early landscapes, done in the 1940s, are thick with paint, like van Gogh's.

Both Burnett and Colville stress how important the passing of time is to an artist, and it is natural for a person in his or her early seventies to reflect on life. I want to pay special attention to retrospection or memory, for it is the *only* way that we can organize the past. Of course, Colville's life and his art look more and more alike in retrospect, but I think that it is his life-long pattern of trying to unite the two to which we should pay attention. That Colville's life has come to look and feel like his pictures does not imply that he has changed the facts of his past to conform with an ideal. Rather, he has always moulded his life after his art and has now brought the two into near-perfect unity.

Whereas most biographies begin at the beginning of their subject's life and work forward chronologically, the past and future implications of Colville's life and work can best be scrutinized retrospectively, according to themes that are crucial over the span of his life. The following sections thus begin from the vantage point of the present and look back. The themes I have chosen are self-presentation, the fragility and affirmation of life, and the art of philosophizing. In selecting these broad headings, I have assumed that most of us know of Colville largely through his art, perhaps from the centennial coins minted in 1967, or from a reproduction of one of his paintings on a book cover. I present his beliefs and passions — in short, what has motivated him to make the readily accessible yet perennially mysterious art for which he has rightly become famous. The result, I hope, is a just picture of Alex Colville's life's work as a tightly organized, complex, ambitious — yet humbly presented — painting.

SELF-PRESENTATION

How does Alex Colville present himself, and why do so many Canadians like him? He admits to being a celebrity: as he puts it in the interview, "People recognize me on airplanes in Canada." He was interviewed on CBC Television's *The National* when his retrospective exhibition opened in Toronto in 1983, he was on

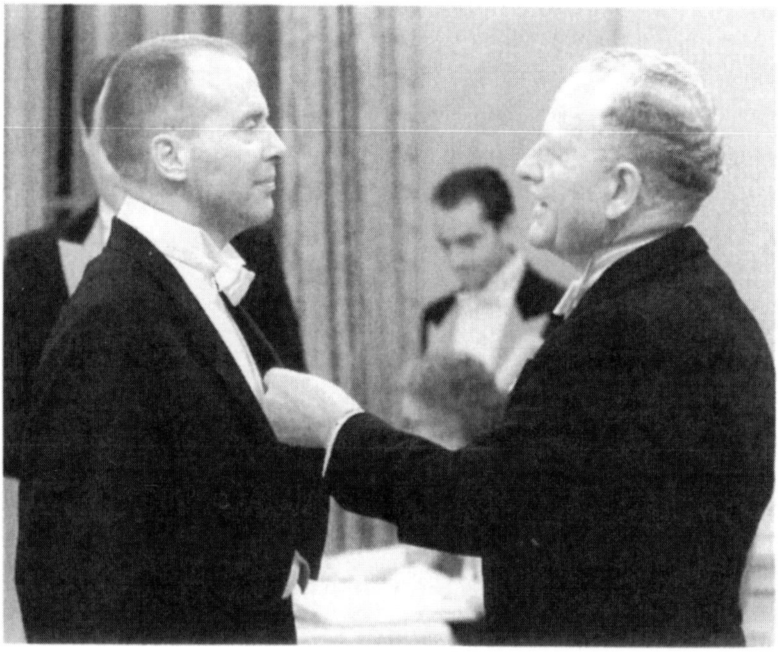

FIGURE 2

Governor General Jules Léger investing Colville as an Officer of the Order of Canada, 1968.

the cover of the 1 August 1983 issue of *Maclean's*, his work was discussed in the August 1975 issue of *Reader's Digest*, and he has received many public honours (see Fig. 2). There was even an attempt — successful, according to the reviews — to adapt his work for the stage.[2] He is as well-known and respected outside the art world as in it. In July 1993, for example, he was made an Honorary Colonel of 415 Maritime Patrol Squadron in Nova Scotia. In fact, he's as likely to be consulted by the media about the Canadian constitution or classical music as he is about his insights into art; indeed, most of us see and hear more of the man than his art. Perhaps celebrity status arrives when one is considered an expert on subjects often well removed from one's true interests or expertise. My point here is not that Colville doesn't have an articulate opinion about the Charlottetown accord of 1992, for example, or about how high-school students should plan their careers. Nor am I suggesting that because he's an artist he should talk only about art. In fact, his activities as a public person — as an authority on life, someone to be listened to and admired — are central to his character and the visibility and significance that he has in Canadian culture. At the same time, Colville is a private man, a detached, though not dispassionate, observer of humanity who has developed a rigorous personal routine in order to make his art. What sort of person is so successful in such different facets of life, and how does he or she get this way?

TWO VIGNETTES

Two vignettes of Colville in public help us to appreciate his complex character. In the first, we see him and his wife Rhoda in the Netherlands at a concert commemorating the forty-fifth anniversary of the liberation of the Netherlands by Canadian troops during World War II. We see Colville talking, after the concert, with Princess Margrethe, sister of the queen of the Netherlands, about his work as an official war artist from 1944–46.

The scene is full of emotion. Colville — typical of the veterans who returned to Europe for this anniversary — has many memories about what he saw in the war, including the horrors at the Belsen concentration camp, which he recorded during a three-day stay in April 1945, and the starvation suffered by the Dutch in the winter of 1945. Rhoda reports that her husband had — and probably still has — nightmares about the war. In another scene, we see the Dutch people and their queen express their abiding gratitude to the former soldier. We learn that Dutch children still tend the thousands of graves of fallen Canadians, and we see Colville moved by this revelation. His presence at this performance in the Het Loo Palace in Apeldoorn encapsulates much of his nature: he is there as both a private person and a veteran. He is there as a former war artist who has become a renowned painter. And he is there as a diplomat, an exemplary Canadian.

These scenes are powerfully presented in the CBC documentary *The Sweetest Spring*, which followed Alex and Rhoda Colville and their granddaughter Ann as they visited the Netherlands in the fall of 1990. The film shows Colville's respect for tradition and continuity, his thoughtfulness about his situation, and his easy movement between his roles as Canadian artist and international diplomat. True to the man, these roles are consciously mixed and blurred in the film. We see Colville's war art, certainly, but it is used largely as a means by which he helps Canadians honour Remembrance Day and the liberation of the Netherlands. The film aired on 8 November 1990, and with it Colville officially became an envoy of Canadians' emotions, someone in whom many of us would like to see ourselves. We are to observe and remember through his able eyes. Even the poignant scenes in which Colville is shown with his young granddaughter — in Anne Frank's house, talking about the teenage girl's bravery in hiding from the Nazis and her death in the Belsen camp, scenes in which the camera skilfully blends Frank's identity with that of Colville's granddaughter as she walks through the house, or in a cemetery, reflecting on "the prospect of dying" — are elevated from personal moments to lessons in life from which we can all learn. Colville presents himself as a person who has something to say, as an artist with insights and values to promote. He projects his values not just to his family or through his work, but universally.

Second vignette: Colville is speaking to about four hundred high-school students at a top secondary institution. He has been invited to speak in the school's Public Affairs Assembly, to be one of a series of speakers who, the organizers hope, will help to acquaint students with the world beyond the classroom. Colville is the first artist to speak in this series, usually reserved for politicians and lawyers. Why *this* artist? One of the student organizers, Richard Pan, responds enthusiastically that Colville is not only a great artist but also a great Canadian, and Pan walked Colville back to his hotel after the lecture to ask for his advice about his own career choices. Again, Colville's public authority springs from his art, yet his art also gains a special aura from his public person.

Colville is clearly at ease in this setting. He likes speaking to general audiences, not only because he sees it as part of his civic duty, but also because he's more comfortable in this context than with other artists. In fact, he actively avoids art contexts, claiming in the interview that he has "never had any desire to meet artists." Moreover, in 1985 Richard Perry quoted him as saying, "I want to live thousands of miles away from other artists. I hate the idea of artists meeting and talking. I don't care what [artists] are doing, I just don't care." Colville is, to say the least, an independent person. He is adept socially, but when it comes to art, he confesses in "Some Observations on My Serigraphs" to having "a very strong aversion to working with other people."

But Colville is happy in front of this group of students. His dry humour isn't lost on his audience: explaining a silkscreen print with "Rat" displayed prominently across the bottom, he quips, "I guess many of you can read," and there is much laughter from a group acclaimed for their academic achievements. But he has a serious message for his young audience, which he states at both the beginning and end of his address. Characterizing himself as a "self-directed person" who has "done what [he] wanted to do," he discusses "the difficulty . . . that young people have in deciding what it is they want to do" in their lives. He stresses that "if you make the right decisions about what you want to do as an adult when you're young, you can end up having quite a good life. If you make the wrong decisions, you can end up possibly having a terrible life." Until Colville utters this last sentence, the students are calmly attentive; when he mentions the weighty responsibility of their choices — the possibility of "a terrible life" — there is nervous laughter. Colville's informal, avuncular manner catches his audience off guard, unprepared for the seriousness of his remarks. He has a habit of telling the worst, of reminding us that evil exists. But he also shows that it can be overcome in moments of what he deems "grace," when the world seems harmonious. Harry Bruce notes that as early as 1967, when Colville addressed a graduating high-school class in Summerside, Prince Edward Island, he surprised parents and students alike by saying, "Sooner or later, but inevitably, you will die. Between now and that final moment, what will you do? How will you live? . . . Life can be most fully lived if we realize that it is finite."

LIFE CHOICES

Colville pictures his own life as a series of mostly good choices. In his address to the students in Toronto, he relates how he decided to become an artist at seventeen, while looking for a university program. He had been offered a scholarship to attend Dalhousie University in Halifax — the result of an essay that he'd submitted for entrance, he notes in "Alex Colville on Alex Colville" — and he considered studying law, he says in his address, because he was intrigued by the idea of becoming a politician; he also thought about attending the Royal Military College in Kingston, Ontario, and "going into the military as a life."

Colville still has a military bearing and personal authority. But encouragement from his first art teacher, Sarah Hart, and from Stanley Royle (1888–1961), a fine arts professor at Mount Allison University in Sackville, New Brunswick, helped him to make up his mind with typical decisiveness and self-understanding. Colville recalls in "Alex Colville on Alex Colville" that Royle saw his talent in Hart's class and arranged a scholarship for him to attend this institution. He also recalls that Dr. B.E. Goodwin, the cultivated physician who treated him when he had pneumonia in 1929, also encouraged him at a crucial time: "knowing him was one of the things that made the idea of becoming an artist legitimate to me much later." Without qualms, then — and partly because he "really didn't want to go . . . and take a B.A.," he says in *Diary of Alex Colville* — he enrolled at Mount Allison and studied under Royle for four years, receiving his Bachelor of Fine Arts degree in 1942.

In "Alex Colville on Alex Colville," he remembers his choice of an artist's life this way:

> When Mr. Royle came over during the winter of my last year of high school, I asked him if he thought I was quite good at drawing and painting and he said "Yes," adding that he thought it was more than just a little talent. I then asked him if he thought that if I became an artist I would be poor and have a terrible time. Fortunately, he said that he didn't think that would happen. I think I decided virtually that same day that I would be an artist.

Colville made this choice with the benefit of support from his parents, a scholarship, and his own talent. His decisiveness was neither impulsive nor facile. In his address, he recalled that his "homeroom teacher" in high school, whom he respected and who had also supported him, thought that he was making "a terrible mistake" in choosing an art career. Yet even at seventeen, Colville knew himself well and undertook the "painful task" of going against his teacher's opinion.

Colville firmly believes in the self-possession that allows one to make choices and avoid "terrible" consequences. He sees his success as the result of self-fashioning: in the interview he says, "You are what you decide you should be; things are sort of wide open. You can decide that you are going to appear to be and live like a plumber's helper, or you can decide you're going to live like someone who is VP of a bank." Colville thinks that the former course — the "plumber's helper" — is the route chosen by most artists; he sees himself as the banker of art. He believes in free will. As he bluntly puts it in my article "The World, the Work, and the Artist," "If you don't like Detroit, get out of Detroit, I would say. People should exercise their wills in these terms more fully perhaps than they do." He has done so, and with great success. He feels sorry for those less fortunate in their career choices, partly because he saw his father — a Scottish immigrant — have to change jobs when he came to Canada and never be satisfied with his career. Colville's older brother Robert, though a professional engineer, had a similar fate in Colville's eyes. The two got on well, but Colville notes in the interview that Robert "should have been a designer" in order to exploit his talents. For the bright and well-situated students at the University of Toronto Schools, to whom he emphasized the importance and possibility of choice, self-determination of his kind is also a real possibility. But even in this group, his remarks caused some discomfort. Are we so free in our choices? Are "we" uniformly able to fashion our lives as Colville would have us do? Or are there people — in Toronto as in Detroit or even in Wolfville — from whom circumstances have stolen what Colville assumes is a basic human characteristic, the ability to choose a life? "I value my absolute freedom and complete independence," John Bentley Mays quotes him as saying. "The only way I could have that is to be economically independent." In promoting the values of self-determination, however, does Colville speak only to a privileged sector of society? Economic independence and strength of will do not always come easily, especially in the 1990s. Yet the appeal of his message lies in its affirmation of our desire and potential to make our lives conform to our choices, just as a finished painting will follow from careful preparatory drawings.

PLANNING IN ART

Colville is famous — even notorious — for the care with which he plans and executes his art works. The choices that he makes in the studio are under his control, and he has created few works outside his own studios, even though he has worked abroad as a visiting artist for significant periods of time (at the University of California, Santa Cruz, in 1967–68, and through the Deutscher Akademischer Austauschdienst [German Academic Exchange Service] in West Berlin for half of 1971). He completes three pieces a year on average,[3] though ideas for his serigraphs and paintings are often in his mind for years. He works through many abstract and then increasingly precise drawings before putting his ideas on a panel in paint, organizing the components of the image within a mathematical system. Rarely does he use photographs: even with the photos of the woman for *French Cross* (1988; Fig. 3), they were, to use his term, "manipulated" and controlled by his memory and subconscious associations. With the exception of a limited series of high-quality photographic reproductions that appeared in 1992, Colville entrusts little to other artists or technicians: he even crafts his own frames.[4] "I am an entrepreneur," he says with typical candour in an interview with Mays. "I make things and I sell them — creative is a word I hate to use. I make the painting, I make the frame in the basement; I ship it off and that's the end of it." His art and working techniques reveal, then, the personal choice and control integral to his character and worldview, and it is instructive to study a painting in which he discloses more directly than usual something of himself, the autobiographical *Target Pistol and Man* (1980; Fig. 4).

Colville turned sixty in 1980, and there is little doubt that this work is partly a response to such a milestone, a demonstration of his thoughts about our progress through life. Colville did several self-portraits as a student, yet Burnett argues that this painting is the only true self-portrait to this date, a doubly important fact because Colville frequently uses his own features in his art. In this unusual work, then, the control gained by using himself as a model is both strengthened and challenged by the forthright vulnerability of such a frank process of self-construction and self-presentation. Burnett further notes that Colville, reflecting on his self-effacement in famous "portraits" such as *Pacific* (1967; Fig. 5) and *Dog and Priest* (1978), exclaimed in 1982, shortly after completing *Target Pistol and Man*, "Why should I always be hiding?" (207).

SELF-EXAMINATION

What does Colville reveal of himself as he comes out of "hiding" in this picture? With typical self-deprecation, he muses in a letter dated 9 September 1987, "in a sense I suppose that as an older man I return to the self-examination or narcissism of youth." We see him as the quintessential observer, gazing at himself in a mirror, the usual technical aid when artists want to portray their features (we know this because his wedding ring appears on his right hand; a photograph would show it on his left, the usual custom in North America). His expression is intense but not tense, a result and record of careful observation. The background is his third-floor studio in his home in Wolfville; aside from this detail and the fact of the self-portrait, there is nothing that shows Colville's profession. Or is there? Self-portraiture is traditionally a vehicle for self-scrutiny. Yet even if we think of artists famous for their work in this genre — Rembrandt (1609–69), van Gogh (1853–90), or the German expressionist Max Beckmann (1884–1950), to whom Colville bears a striking physical resemblance, and whose numerous self-portraits, including one made when Beckmann turned sixty, "I have always been interested in," Colville says in my article — it is also the place to project an ideal self-image. In *Target Pistol and Man*, even

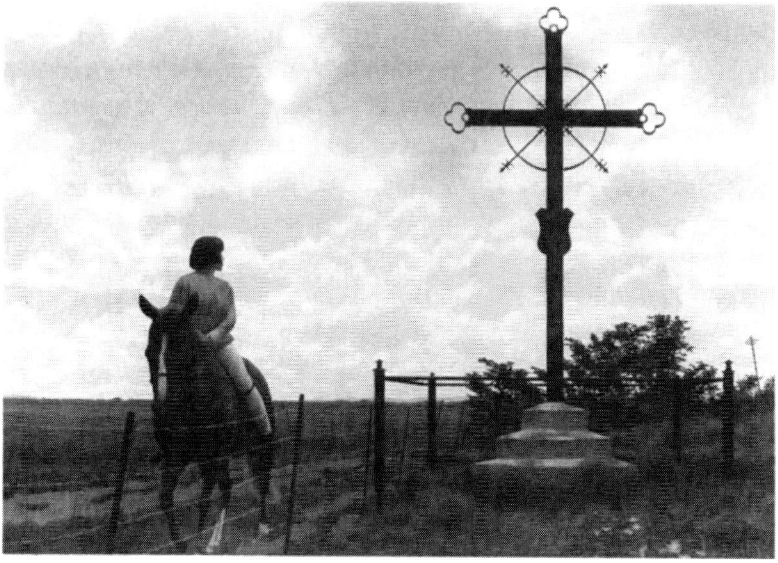

FIGURE 3

Colville, French Cross *(1988): acrylic on particle board, 56.5 x 80 cm., private collection.*

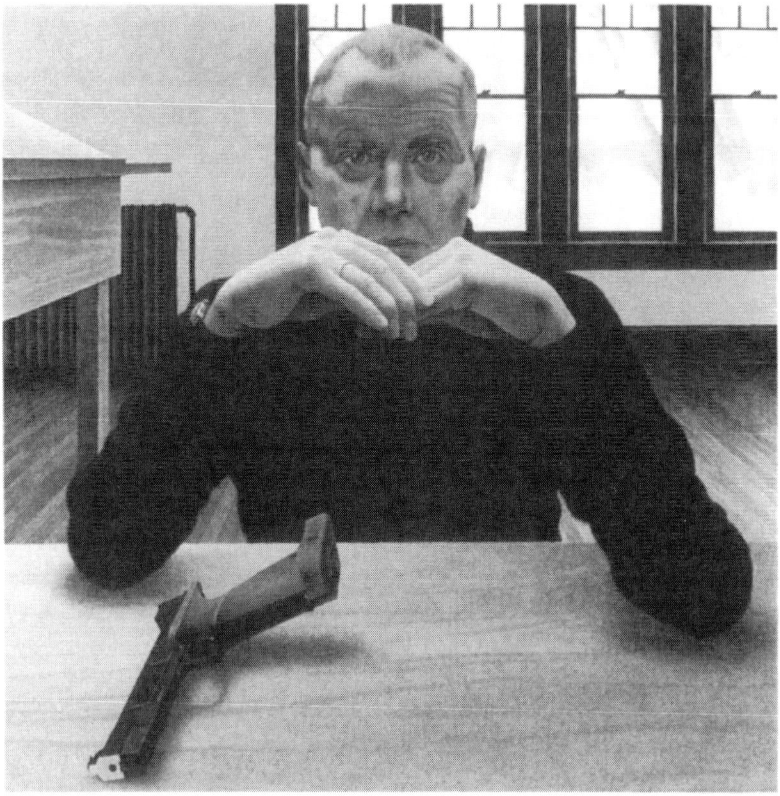

FIGURE 4

Colville, Target Pistol and Man *(1980): acrylic polymer emulsion, 60 x 60 cm., private collection.*

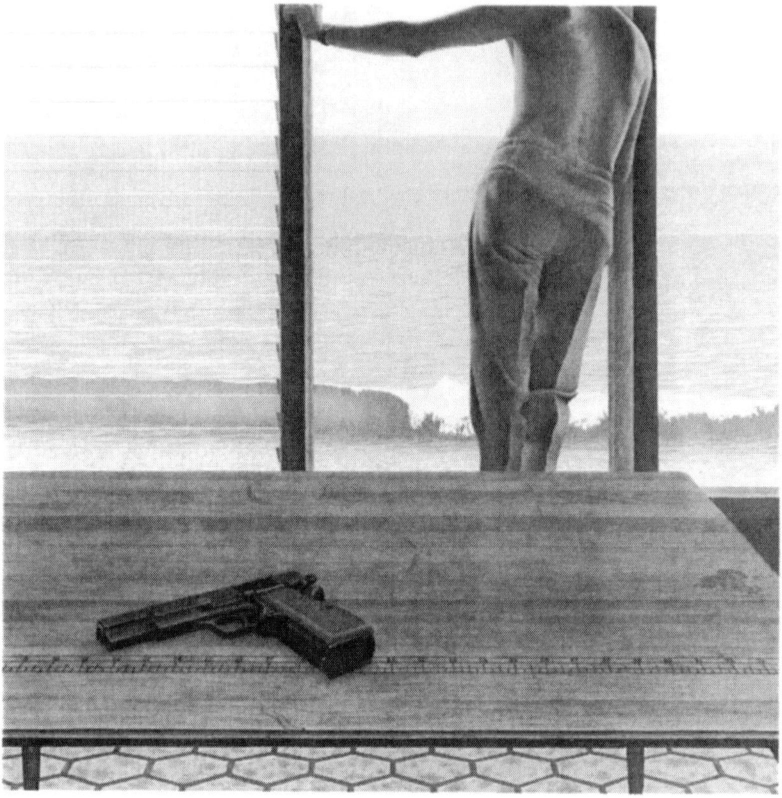

FIGURE 5

Colville, Pacific *(1968): acrylic polymer emulsion, 53.3 x 53.3 cm., private collection.*

with its anonymous, universalizing title, Colville shows us his own closely studied face and the spare surroundings in which he likes to work. His precision in rendering them earns his work the label "realism." With the unsettling inclusion of the pistol on the table before the man, he also exploits self-portraiture's ability to convey its artist's desired self-image, the self-fashioning so characteristic of Alex Colville. The title tells us that this gun is a "target pistol" that the "man" can use to test his hand-and-eye coordination. Colville has belonged to a gun club for years, so for him this pistol isn't primarily a weapon. On the contrary, it is an incarnation of the life-affirming precision and control that he strives for in his life and work, as he also shows in a painting entitled *Target Shooting* (1990), in which a father checks with binoculars his son's accuracy at a target-shooting range. For Colville, though perhaps not for all of us, *Target Pistol and Man* is not an image of potential violence; the contemplation of suicide or murder means, for him, a lack of self-control, the antithesis of what his art and life are about.

At sixty, then, Colville accentuated the precision of his life and work with this haunting self-portrait. More than anything, it is an image of corporeal and psychological observation. Colville is rigorous in his attention to physiognomic detail, yet his hands and eyes are subtly exaggerated. Interestingly his hands partly obscure his mouth; this mannerism is even more evident in the powerful black-and-white photograph of Colville by Arnaud Maggs that is the frontispiece in Burnett's study and that hangs over Colville's desk in his office, adjacent to his studio. In this portrait, Colville's folded hands cover his mouth completely, making his calm but penetrating eyes more searching. By placing his hands this way in situations in which he has considerable control over the image, Colville isn't simply attending to the truth of an observed situation. He is consciously performing the role of a particular sort of visual artist, one who doesn't speak in the first instance but rather looks and then makes his statement with his hands, a statement in turn addressed to our eyes and minds. Colville is profoundly interested in literature and well-read, but he is not a writer. As he notes in his address to the University of Toronto Schools audience, if he were a poet, then he would read poetry to them: "If you could put words" to the work, "you wouldn't have to do the painting." Because he's a visual artist, he shows them the fruits of his vision. "But the real answer which someone who is trying to be an artist gives," Colville asserts in his "Statement," is "wordlessly, silently, imbedded in the work which that person does."

Colville also remarks in this address that most of his portraits — whether of himself or others — are "obscured." He specifically refers to the 1991 painting *Chaplain*, in which a clerical friend is pictured through the spindles of a pulpit railing. I think that *all* of Colville's portraits are "obscured" in that their directness and detail magnify rather than remove our sense of wonder at what is being presented. His visual precision shows us less than we might think; much is left for us to see with the *mind's* eye. *Dog and Groom* (1991), for example — in which he portrays himself in his home, combing his dog — shows us much about Colville, the room, and the dog. Again his hands and eyes are emphasized, habitually working to keep life in order. Yet it is the dog's eyes that look benevolently at us; Colville's gaze is on his task, and his body is partly obscured by the dog's. As in *Target Pistol and Man*, we see a universalized moment (to distance himself from his earlier work, Colville not only gave it a characteristically laconic title but also left his signature off the front of the panel), but behind this screen of anonymity, we see Colville's own values. He celebrates order, precision, and control. Even when he captures himself in an apparently casual activity — grooming his dog, studying himself in a mirror, or in an informal photo that graced the cover of *Canadian Art* magazine in the fall of 1987, in which he looks out at us through a partly opened screen door that he holds with a hand made prominent by its proximity to the camera and which in turn partly covers his face — Colville masks his identity yet magnifies his hands and eyes, the vehicles of his art. In doing so, he reveals much of his character, for he doesn't want a cult of personality but rather the feeling of mystery and strangeness that his images leave with so many of their viewers.

The qualities projected by Colville in *Target Pistol and Man* (Fig. 4) are at one with his public persona in the vignettes I have described: he is an observer and a maker, and he embodies planning and precision in his choices. He is direct and honest, but he doesn't spell everything out. He holds views with passion and confidence, yet he is undogmatic, curious to know more about the world. If we ask how Colville acquired these traits, we must inevitably question the balance of nature and nurture, of how much of his personality he was simply born with and how much developed because of formative experiences. I will not attempt to determine the proportion of each element: Colville displays a seemingly innate authority and integrity, yet some of his experiences have also shaped him considerably. I will instead consider two phases of his life that were especially crucial: his time in the Canadian army and as a war artist (1942–46), and his subsequent career as a university art teacher (1946–63).

IN THE ARMY

Colville enlisted in the Canadian army in May 1942, a month before his graduation from Mount Allison. Burnett states that he hoped to become a war artist and thus to continue his work (40): he had been encouraged to follow this path by Colonel A.F. Duguid, head of the army's Historical Section, who knew his work from a poster that the young artist had done for the Wartime Information Bureau. Even though the war artists' program wouldn't be approved until January 1943, Colville knew that he needed to become an officer to have any chance at the position. Hence, he enrolled for training at Brockville. Burnett notes that he was rejected — for being "too independent-minded," as Colville subsequently put it (40) — and spent the next two years working through the ranks at camps in Fredericton, Petawawa (near Ottawa), and elsewhere. He finally received his commission in September 1943. Colville became an infantry second lieutenant and trained other soldiers. He had no time for art, and, for the duration of the war, virtually gave up the idea of bettering himself in this area. He was happy enough, though, especially because he had married Rhoda Wright — a fellow fine arts student whom he had met in university — in August 1942, and they were together. Their relatively tranquil existence was to end abruptly.

Colville recalls the change in "Alex Colville on Alex Colville":

> Suddenly I was sent overseas in a very dramatic way. My wife and I were living in a little place in a camp near Yarmouth, Nova Scotia. The assistant adjutant arrived at our home in a jeep, and said the Colonel wanted to see me. . . . As soon as I got there the Colonel said, "You're leaving at 3:45 on a Canso aircraft and you're being flown to Halifax and Montreal and England," then he said, "Mr. Churchill wants you." I didn't know what it was all about. When I got to London, I was told to report to Canadian Military H.Q., to a Colonel C.P. Stacey and he said, "You've been made a war artist."

Apparently Colonel Duguid hadn't forgotten Colville, even though, Burnett notes, the civilian war art advisory panel — which included H.O. McCurry, Charles Comfort, and A.Y. Jackson — didn't recommend him (40).[5] Colville wasn't given time to ponder his good fortune or consider the role of a war artist. In "War Diary and Other Recollections," he recalls that Colonel Stacey simply said, "You must remember you are no longer an infantry officer. I don't want you getting killed," and sent him off to work with a supply unit in Yorkshire. "I was given water-colours, five pens and I went up there," Colville remembers; "it seemed wonderful to be painting again."[6]

Most important from today's perspective is what Colville made of his new position and how it affected his character and art, his worldview. In a typically matter-of-fact way, he describes, during a 1980 interview contained in "War Diary," how he

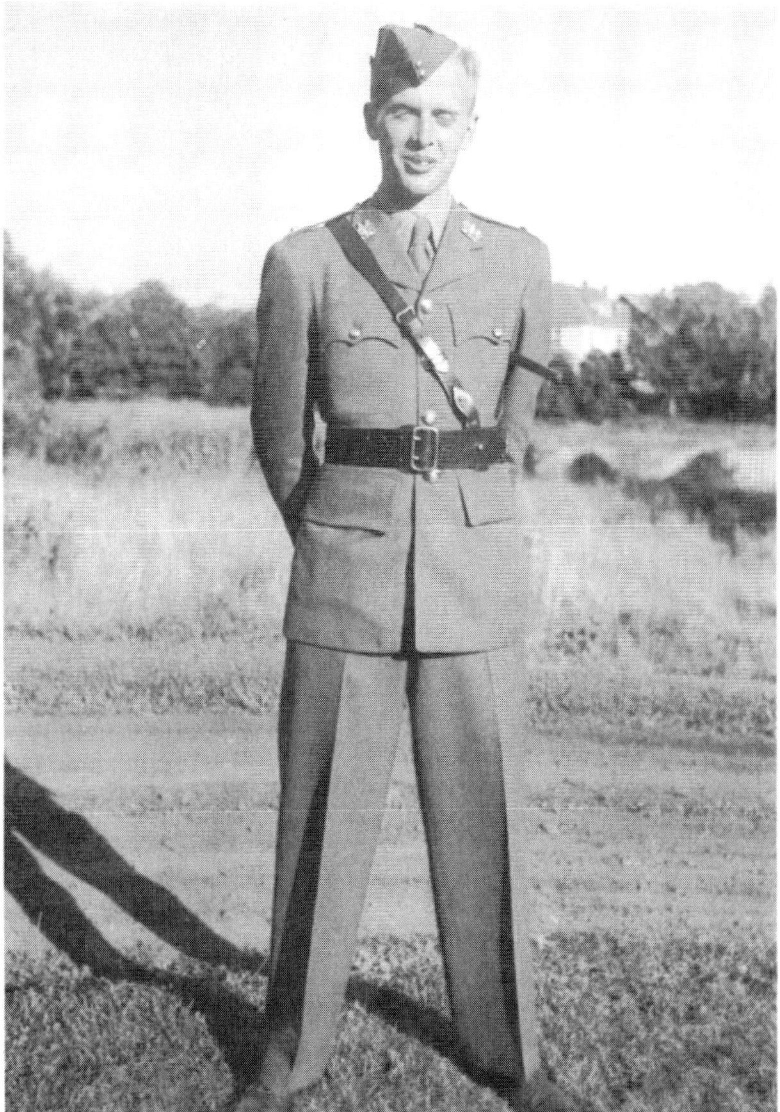

FIGURE 6

Colville, commissioned second lieutenant in the Canadian army, Amherst, Nova Scotia, September 1943.

viewed his new task: "I simply thought I will do something each day. If it's good, fine; if it isn't good, that's too bad. There aren't too many situations in which a very young painter . . . is encouraged to work every day, and I was. It was a great thing." He has elaborated on this description by comparing himself to a famous writer: "I was like Hemingway," Mays quotes him as saying, "who worked as a journalist to support his art. I was doing stuff day after day, like a young writer doing his thousand words a day." Much of Colville's wartime diary is devoted to artistic matters, both technical and philosophical. From his reflections we gain valuable insight into his ideas and priorities in life. Remarking on the differences between his work as a visual artist and the work of the Canadian filmmakers and photographers, for example, he claimed that

> the camera can record, can make extraordinarily good, affecting records, but a painter is more likely to select and reject, to edit, to interpret. You are not a camera, you are doing essentially different things. . . . I wasn't a mature artist. I was a young, bright person. I had been a good student, and I was technically competent. I considered my job essentially to record.

So record he did, almost every day for two years, working mostly outdoors with pen and watercolour: "I would go out with this jeep and driver. Anything I saw that was kind of interesting I would make a drawing or a watercolour of it. So it was a kind of genre painting of everyday life in the army." Colville travelled widely to capture this quotidian existence — first with the navy in the Mediterranean, then in Belgium, the Netherlands, and Germany with the Third Canadian Infantry Division. The only artist assigned to this group of approximately fifteen thousand soldiers, he had enough freedom to set his own routine — unusual in the army — and his pattern of daily work has remained unchanged (except that the jeep has been replaced by somewhat faster — and usually German — transportation) for nearly fifty years. The army suited Colville, partly because he had more independence than most of his peers, but also because it provided intriguing subject matter for his art. Colville has always loved machines. His recollections of his early art attest to his passion: he notes in "Alex Colville on Alex Colville" that at nine, "the drawings I did were all of machines, without exception. I drew cars, boats, airplanes, things like that." A great deal of his war art focuses on the machinery of armed conflict — tanks, airplanes, ships, and especially bridges (see Fig. 7) — with little attention to the human subject. His recent work demonstrates his continuing interest in machines: *Traveller* (1992; Fig. 8) pictures the view from inside Colville's own Porsche 911; *Couple on Bridge* (1992) features the complex structure of a bridge, a "machine" that Colville learned to appreciate as a boy because his father was a steelworker on bridges (see Fig. 9), and which he thematized during the war, as his many pictures of the strategic bridge at Nijmegen, in the Netherlands, attest (see Fig. 7). We see in *The Sweetest Spring* that Colville made a pilgrimage to this bridge when he returned to the Netherlands in 1990.

THE EVERYDAY WAR

Colville took the representation of war seriously. His was a special sort of interpretation, a communication on behalf of the soldiers. As he noted in "War Diary,"

> In a certain sense I was writing letters home for these people, depicting their lives, the dugouts, tanks, where they lived. I was making a kind of record. There is always this element in art. "Life is short, but art is long." A lot of these people were killed. They would be very interested in what I was doing, kind of astonished at it in a way.

Colville relates in *The Sweetest Spring* that a senior officer to whom he had shown his work — Major General D.C. Spry,

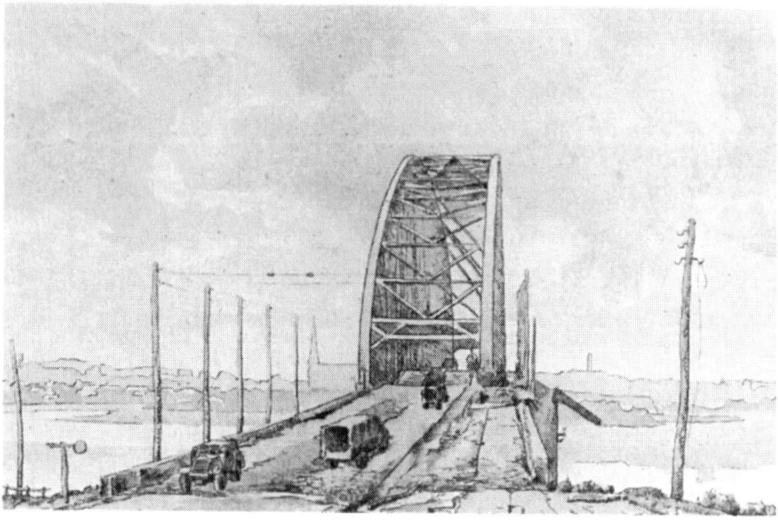

FIGURE 7

Colville, Nijmegen Bridge — Late Afternoon *(15 Nov. 1944): pen and watercolour on paper, 31.6 x 45.6 cm., collection of the Canadian War Museum.*

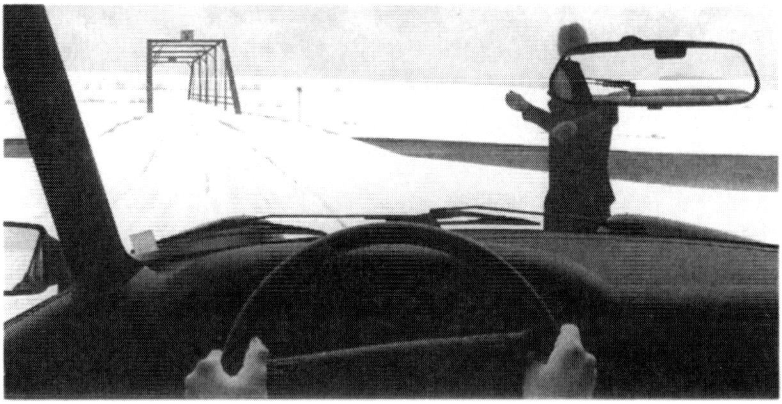

FIGURE 8

Colville, Traveller *(1992): acrylic on particle board, 43.2 x 86.4 cm., collection of The Drabinsky Gallery.*

commander of the 3rd Canadian Infantry Division — noticed how soldiers struggled to portray "the reality of war" in their letters home. As Colville explains in a letter dated 4 June 1993, Spry knew the limits of most soldiers' powers of self-expression. The war artist's images were designed to help them picture this reality. Colville's war art thus gave him early and intense experience in seeing for others, an experience that has influenced his outlook and subsequent art in important ways.

While Colville is acutely aware of the passage of time and change, he is also convinced of the permanence of art: as he puts it, "Life is short, but art is long." His art is typically about everyday occurrences with which he is intimately familiar and it testifies to what is, for him, the ultimate importance of these things, just as his war art does. While he has consistently pictured scenes that may seem uninteresting or unimportant, he claims that he doesn't find this level of reality banal. The war not only gave him valuable practice in the technical side of art; it also gave the young Colville a sense of belonging — even psychological security — *as* an artist, a sense that is crucial to him. As he notes in "War Diary,"

> There was no resentment. Most artists of this century are said to feel estranged from society; that is, they feel that they're a kind of outcast, that people don't understand them. It is said there is a gap, that there is a barrier between the artist and society in general. Well, you see through this experience as a war artist. I never felt much of this gap business. I didn't feel that I was misunderstood or not sufficiently appreciated.

Today Colville casts himself as a banker rather than a "starving artist," as someone who is a pillar of society rather than on its margins. He doesn't see himself as an outcast or critic: he prefers to be — and is — in the centre of his society, even in its corridors of power. That he enjoyed his role as a war artist, however, says more about Colville than about the "gap" between society and the artist; there are simply different types of artists, and people react differently to these types. Some are thus critical of Colville's corporate profile, while others are attracted to it. In the interview, he comments on the negative reaction to his public image: "Normally people who are in the arts slot themselves in with what I would call the proletariate, and I don't. People find this baffling, and maybe irritating."

Colville's detached observation of what surrounded the soldiers in World War II, as well as the world in which he now lives, is fundamental to his way of being in the world. Although he did see action in the war — and vividly recalls an assault in the Mediterranean in which he took part — he has always tended to celebrate the routine. "It's very difficult to describe what war is like," he says in "War Diary." "Much of nothing happen[s]." But this does not mean that the "nothing" — the waiting, the machinery, the preparation for war, or, now, the trip to the post office — is unimportant. Indeed, to Colville, familiar daily activities are what make it possible for many people to identify with his work. Thus in *Nijmegen Bridge — Late Afternoon* (see Fig. 7), a pen-and-watercolour drawing done in 1944, we see the famous and strategic bridge, but at a normal moment, not one chosen for its drama.

BELSEN

It's worth asking — as a counterpoise to the order that Colville tries to maintain in his life and environment — how he reacts to extraordinary or unsettling events. Both during and since the war, Colville has avoided such emotional situations. Images such as *Berlin Bus* (1978), in which a young woman is shown running full tilt beside a bus, or *Skater* (1964), in which the woman's movements are carefully controlled by the artist's mathematical composition, are the exceptions that prove the rule that Colville patterns his life and art to avoid unusual experiences. But what about events in which he had to participate, such as his visit to the Belsen concentration camp in 1945? Colville's diary entry, made at the time, is telling:

> On 29 April I drove to this camp at Belsen, saw the authorities there, was dusted (as a protection against typhus) and set up camp in a nearby barracks. That afternoon I visited No. 1 concentration camp. I will make no attempt to describe the conditions there as they have already been adequately described by others. The subjects were not of a sort which can be executed expressively at the time, on the spot. I felt that I would get the most out of this visit by making sketches, then returning to these sketches at some later time. On the first day I made a drawing of some women, dead from starvation and typhus, lying outside one of the huts. While I drew, the group of bodies was added to as more people died and were feebly dragged out of the hut by the inhabitants, who were themselves more dead than alive. On 30 April it rained all morning. In the afternoon I began a watercolour of one of the huge open graves, with the camp in the background. I finished this the next morning. This afternoon I made a drawing of bodies lying in a grave. These were soon obscured by other bodies which were being thrown from the back of a truck.

Colville's description is typically terse, and Perry notes that his responses, both written and painted, can be criticized for their "emotional sterility or at least reticence." Colville does distance himself emotionally. On the one hand, in the face of such cruelty and suffering, who wouldn't? On the other hand, aren't Perry and others who seek a witness to such travesties entitled to more than a matter-of-fact description?

Removed considerably from the experience, Colville reflected, during a 1980 interview contained in "War Diary,"

> This being at Belsen was strange[;] . . . one felt badly that one didn't feel worse. That is to say, you see one dead person and it is too bad, but seeing five hundred is not five hundred times worse. There is a certain point at which you begin to

feel nothing. . . . It was a profoundly affecting experience. Obviously it would be, unless a person was an absolute fool.

Is Colville here revealing the truth of his self-characterization, in Perry's article, as "a cold fish," or is he just being honest about his inability to feel completely the enormity (in both senses of the term) of what he saw at Belsen? Perry claims that Colville's reactions in the camp are of a piece with his later aversion to the depiction of human emotion, witnessed by Colville's "preference [for] . . . averted faces" in his art during and since the war. If we have a right to judge Colville here — and this itself is an issue, especially because many of us who read Colville's words or see his images did not experience the Holocaust — then we must weigh his statements and images against other possible, and more overtly emotional, responses and concerns. About the war, Colville claims in "War Diary" that its "immediacy had a philosophical effect on me." Although he remarked in "My Experience as a Painter and Some General Views of Art" (1951) that he was "bewildered" "by the lack in me of [a] total concept of the war, or . . . a clear attitude toward the war," he has since developed "philosophical" responses about the human capacity for evil. Bruce quotes him as saying, for example, "I didn't really know what to think about the Germans. . . . But I have the feeling that they've faced certain things that other people haven't. . . . They were the first to find out how terrible people — I mean *they* and others — can be." More pungently, he claims in Mays's article that "The Germans have this feeling, and I think they are right, that things can go to hell in a minute. Canadians are unbelievably naive about their capacity for evil." Colville doesn't think that wars will cease, nor does he overestimate the role of war artists: as he notes in "War Diary," "I can't see that war art serves any moral function in depicting the horrors of war." Yet he still thinks about the war, and is outspoken about *The Valour and the Horror*, a recent and controversial CBC Television documentary that shows the less heroic sides of Canada's involvement in World War II, notably the bombing of civilians by

Canadian and other Allied air forces. To Colville the war veteran, this film is "the work of a . . . second-rate mind. What I see in it is sociological clap-trap," he says in the interview. These aren't the words of an unemotional bystander, but Colville's proclivity is for philosophical formulations rather than immediate emotional involvement. We see this trait in his diary writings and art alike. For some this is a vice; for others it is a virtue. Whether we agree with him about the CBC film, or are attracted or repulsed by his way of showing the war, depends largely on our traits and those that we ascribe to him.

For Colville, as for most soldiers, the war years were a time of vivid experience and maturation. Perhaps more than many of his peers, Colville knew who he was and behaved according to his self-image. Nonetheless his war diary records a few uncharacteristic lapses in judgement. On shore leave in Italy while he was seconded to the navy, Colville attended an opera; he writes: "Went to Opera in the afternoon saw 'Tosca.' Was ready to leave after first act but 2nd and 3rd were better. I have no desire to see another opera. I believe that Italians are incapable of producing any vital art." Perhaps he had succumbed to anti-Italian war propaganda, but there is something remarkably consistent in Colville's disliking of opera here. What he reacted against in opera so long ago is the same dramatic quality that he finds distasteful in the work of the famous painter El Greco (1541–1614) and baroque and Catholic Reformation art in general. He notes in "The World" that "It seems too theatrical and phony." Referring to the work of the well-known Canadian portrait photographer Yousuf Karsh, Colville is equally derisive: his "stuff tends to look [too] theatrical," he says in the interview. Put another way, Colville disapproves of performance. He likes work that is fashioned rationally, like "ancient Egyptian sculpture . . . and the paintings of Seurat. . . . These were things that weren't performed works of art but which were built works . . ." he says in *Diary*. Consistency aside, though, both Alex and Rhoda Colville now find his overly confident pronouncement about Italian art most amusing.

As we have seen, the major lines of Colville's character and art were evident while he was a war artist. During this time, he gained confidence in his chosen vocation. In early 1945, for example, he recorded something of a conceptual breakthrough. "I envisaged my first big canvas," he reports in "War Diary" with more enthusiasm than usual, "the subject being infantry marching in a single file along a road." He did drawings for this work on the spot, and then worked up the idea into a full-scale oil painting when he (along with the other Canadian war artists) had a studio in Ottawa immediately after his return from overseas. The result—*Infantry, Near Nijmegen, Holland* (1946)—is one of Colville's best-known works. We see a line of troops stretching into the misty distance. The men nearest to us are close and rendered in detail. We see their faces clearly, but all have their eyes averted; they appear weary, lost in thought or marching on automatic pilot. Again, Colville shows the emptiness and tedium of war, not its drama or the heroism of its combatants.

RETURN TO CANADA

Colville's routine had been abruptly broken when he was sent to England to become a war artist; his return to Canada was equally an occasion when he was flooded with emotion. As he says in "War Diary,"

> I came home on the ISLE DE FRANCE with 11,000 other people. We sailed into Halifax harbour on a Sunday morning, the 21st of October [1945]. It was a very beautiful morning, clear and sunny. I had never thought of myself as a patriot or even as a sentimental person, but I was very moved by this experience.

Colville returned to Rhoda and their first son, Graham, who had been born over a year earlier, in July 1944, while his father was in Europe. There are diary entries about Colville buying things for

Graham, but this was their first meeting. War artists were expected to produce more than drawings and watercolours. In fact, the normal procedure was for the artist to have a studio in London, England, from time to time in order to make oil paintings based on field work. Circumstances gave Colville almost no time to do this, so he was fortunate to spend his final months in the army in Ottawa, sharing a studio with other returning artists. He was demobilized in June 1946 at the rank of captain.

The months following his return must have been both exhilarating and stressful for Colville, as for many of the returning soldiers. He was reunited with his family, and his work was going well. It was generally a time of optimism, of looking to a brighter future. Colville recalls in the interview that it was in this spirit that he joined the Canadian Legion in Sackville, even donating to it one of his war pieces: he thought, "now, all these people are veterans, there's a chance to do something." But his high hopes were soon disappointed: "I then realized after going to a few Legion meetings that in fact what people did was just sit around and talk about football or golf. [So] I just sort of drifted out of it." Why was Colville so discouraged? Young-Bruel writes that in "the years immediately after World War II, . . . an atmosphere of passionate quest invisibly united intellectuals in all the lands . . . torn by the war; a quest to understand what had happened. . . ." Colville was and is an intellectual, concerned with literature, philosophy, and the big questions in life. As we've seen, he wanted to make sense of the war in his own terms, and he wanted to help rebuild a culture so depleted by the war. He was committed and idealistic, but not everyone shared his passion for building a future. In fact, he found that most people were only coping with material reality. "I was shocked when I got home," he recalls in the interview with some animation, "that we couldn't find a place to live!" Rhoda and Graham thus returned to her family home in Wolfville and were apart from Alex for a time. We can understand his frustration. Fortunately his enthusiasm and desire to move forward were not thwarted for long.

Colville was naturally thinking about how to maintain his fledgling career as an artist without his army position. Commercial art was an option. University teaching was another, one that offered him the relative calm and solitude that he craved after the war. The latter alternative in effect chose him, though he was also encouraged by Will Ogilvie, an artist and friend. Colville received an offer to teach in the Fine Arts Department at Mount Allison University, the institution and department from which he had graduated only four years earlier. Not one to hesitate, and in need of financial security, Colville took the job immediately. He began teaching in the fall of 1946 and would have worked with his former mentor, Stanley Royle, except that Royle had left Canada in October 1945, the month that Colville returned. Nonetheless "I had a very teacher/apprentice sort of relationship" with him, Colville recalls fondly in the interview. He still admires Royle's work.

At the start at least, "University life was quite wonderful . . . ," Colville further recalls, largely because about a quarter of the class was comprised of veterans, older, more serious students with whom he had an easy rapport: "We had a very close connection; this was a very small group of students. It was almost like being in the army, it was like having a platoon." Colville was now training artists instead of soldiers, as he had done as a young officer. One of his former students, London, Ontario, artist Roly Fenwick (who hadn't been in the war), corroborates this picture of the good relations between the fine arts students and their new professor. He recalls Colville's classes in the early 1950s, when students and teacher would exchange cigarettes and talk about life beyond the classroom. All seemed to be going well for Colville at Mount Allison, yet if we read his 1951 artist's statement, or read too much into his resignation in 1963, we might wonder about his enthusiasm for teaching. In November 1951, speaking at the opening of his exhibition at the New Brunswick Museum in St. John, Colville the teacher stated (somewhat theatrically, as we read it now in "My Experience"),

> . . . I had always felt dislike and even contempt for the teaching profession. . . . There is, of course, a very real danger in teaching for an artist. With every succeeding year he becomes, by comparison with the students, more experienced, more adept in intellectual and technical procedures, and this process is likely to menace and finally overwhelm two qualities which are essential to an artist — the sense of humility and the sense of mystery.

We can tell much about Colville from his attitudes here and from his thinking about teaching generally. Clearly he was concerned to do a good job as a teacher (this sense of responsibility typified his attitude to his war art, and is a constant in his character). By 1951, five years into his teaching career, Colville also sensed that he was moving ahead as an artist, and that his growing sophistication might make him a less effective teacher. We also see from this passage that he is a good storyteller, less averse to dramatizing his life and ideas than to the theatricality typical of opera. Hyperbole, irony, and a wry sense of humour attend his putative "contempt for the teaching profession." Colville also has a way of explaining himself with seemingly tangential but usually revealing anecdotes. For example, "thinking of my own children," he reflects in "A Tribute to Professor George P. Grant," "I have thought what a blessing it is that the young, including university students, pay so little attention to their teachers that the influence of bad teachers seems to be negligible."

Asked recently about his distaste for teaching, he says laughingly in the interview, "It's not really true" and then tells a story about his first experiences in school. "I was left handed. The teacher was a woman . . . who I thought of as an attractive woman. On the second day of class [she offered a prize of cookies] . . . to everyone who wrote well, and of course I did not write well because I was writing with my right hand," as students were obliged to do at that time. This failure to impress someone whom he admired was an "early experience that always rankled with me," and he took a serious lesson from it: "you must not expect much from the education system!", a system that more often than not tries to force one into an ill-fitting mould. We shouldn't assume that Colville's later feelings about teaching stem from this incident — he continues to be left-handed — but the fact that he recalls it over sixty-five years later can't be overlooked.

TEACHING ART HISTORY

More generally, his position as a teacher wasn't always as ideal as the first years seem in retrospect. Like many new teachers, he found little time to do any work that wasn't related to teaching. In his first four years at Mount Allison, he produced little, even by his steady but less than prolific standards, and he wasn't pleased with his paintings until about 1950. Colville initially taught drawing and introductory art history, and he now thinks that teaching art history might have been more important to him than teaching art: "I was learning from it as a painter," he says. Because he wasn't formally trained in art history, he was learning along with his students, keeping just ahead of them. He had been overwhelmed by a visit to the Louvre at the end of the war. Now he was going through art history systematically — using texts by Helen Gardner and E.H. Gombrich — and discovering kindred spirits, it seems, in the tranquillity of ancient Egyptian art and early Italian Renaissance painting. He included his students in what he was discovering about past art. For example, he would find colour illustrations in *Life* and *Time* magazines to show them (this was before the widespread classroom use of colour slides). He even asked a local company for cardboard on which to mount these images for his students' use. Another anecdote shows how Colville's experience with art history in a studio arts program has led to a principle about art education. At the University of

Toronto Schools lecture in 1992, Colville answered a student's question about the best path to choose to become an artist by relating a story about the contemporary Saskatchewan sculptor Joe Fafard, who once told him that the only art teacher who had given him anything valuable had been the art history teacher. Colville's lesson is that an artist always starts from past art.

Colville sums up his feelings about his teaching at Mount Allison directly in the interview: "I liked teaching, and I think I was a good teacher." His central idea about teaching is encapsulated in a remark about the French thinker Albert Camus and Colville's friend, the Canadian philosopher George Grant. Attending one of Colville's slide lectures in the 1970s, Grant, Colville recalls in "A Tribute," "listened, and presumably looked, in the way that a few good students do, in that open and vulnerable way. (When Camus first came to New York after the second war an acute observer said his essential characteristic was vulnerability.) I think George's students realized that he was learning while teaching — including learning from them." Even though he has strong convictions, Colville also has this look of vulnerability, the sensitivity to realize that the world is bigger than he is.

Colville the teacher has influenced a number of artists, many of whom see him in a way that he doesn't see himself, as the leader of a realist school of Canadian painters. A feeling among former students, however, is that Colville wasn't so good in class. Emphasizing that Colville was "always very good to me," and a model *outside* the classroom, Fenwick makes a distinction between the tone of Colville's art-history classes, which he remembers as rather "austere, stern," and the studio sessions, in which Colville was more relaxed and clearly in his element. In the art history classes, Colville was, he says, very academic, telling no jokes and heeding protocol. Just back from the war, perhaps he took the "platoon" idea too literally, and, of course, he was new at teaching art history. Fenwick and others learned as much from his example as a man and artist — from 1946–58 he had his studio at the university — as from his teaching.

Colville's unique charisma drew people to him, and made him an influential authority on life as much as art. Even as a self-styled inexperienced student, Fenwick recalls feeling that he was in the presence of someone who would become a great artist.

University teachers were not paid well in the 1940s and 1950s, but the position gave the Colvilles enough security to have more children: John was born in July 1946; Charles in February 1948; and Ann in August 1949 (see Fig. 11). "Being the child of an artist is tough," Colville reminisces in the interview. "[My] work was very demanding and time consuming. I didn't spend as much time [with the family] as perhaps I should have." Perhaps most difficult is that "The father is thought of as something of a freight by most people," by which Colville means that he was in a way a burden to his children because he didn't have a nine-to-five job but did have notoriety beginning in the mid-1960s, when television programs about him began to appear. Colville was not only an artist, of course, but also a faculty member, a professor with both administrative and teaching duties. Although he enjoyed being in a university and interacting with people from other disciplines — particularly Philosophy — Colville complains in the interview that "the political side of university life was really terrible, just awful." Furthermore, Burnett says in a personal interview that Colville "still speaks about some of the personalities [at Mount Allison] with a certain sense of rancour." Not one to shrink from his duty to his institution, however, Colville was very involved with university politics for a time. More than anything else, these ultimately negative experiences led him to resign in 1963. As he puts it with typical bluntness in 1989 in "A Tribute," "I . . . decided, in February 1963 . . . that I could not stay in a university because I found some of my colleagues literally intolerable."

One sore point was his relationship with the head of the Fine Arts Department, another artist, Lawren P. Harris (1910–), who had been appointed head at the same time that Colville was hired. Harris is the son of the famous Lawren S. Harris (1885–1970), perhaps the best-known member of the Group of Seven.

The Harris family was wealthy and aristocratic, and one of Colville's earliest memories of his future boss, he says in the interview, was "actually defending [him] in a group, saying, 'Well, the guy is from the Massey-Harris family and everything, and that's not his fault.'" Colville had known Harris slightly when both were war artists, and he liked some of his war art. Colville also has respect for those with social standing, for aristocrats. Working together at Mount Allison, however, "was a very difficult thing," and "we in fact didn't get on very well." Part of the problem was that Harris, the older man with seniority, taught both studio and art history classes to the upper-level students. Colville didn't think that Harris was qualified: "Although he had some kind of talent as a painter, the thing was that he had virtually no education." Dennis Reid notes that Harris attended the School of the Boston Museum of Fine Arts in 1931–32, but he had no university degree, as Colville did. Harris also disapproved of Colville maintaining a studio in the department, even though students liked the idea. Fenwick recalls how important the example of an artist at work in his studio was to his own career. To many of the students, Harris was an overbearing person, and, to make things worse, he lived right across the street from the Colvilles in Sackville. This difficult interaction, Colville (in a temperate mood) says in the interview, "made it more necessary for me to resign when I did."

Another "political" aspect of university work that Colville was good at but came to dislike was administration. In the late 1950s, still wanting to change things as he had when he returned from Europe over a decade earlier, Colville was active in the new faculty association at Mount Allison. Early in 1959, at the request of the president, he became the chair of a new committee founded to study whether Mount Allison should expand. Colville remembers many meetings with the four other members of this important committee. Over the Easter break in 1959, he wrote a draft of the committee's recommendation that Mount Allison *not* expand. This advice was accepted by the senior administration, and Colville still feels good about the decision to keep Mount Allison small. In comparison, he points to the growing pains suffered by Acadia University in Wolfville, which chose the opposite course.

LEAVING TEACHING

Soon after his administrative success, Colville became president of the faculty association. One of his duties was to chair another new committee, rather imposingly named The Committee on Excellence, given a mandate in the fall of 1961 to design a blueprint for the future of the university, one that would both generate for, and solicit from, the faculty ideas on a range of issues and, ideally, guide the new president then being sought. He and nine colleagues on the committee submitted "The Idea of Excellence at Mount Allison" in May 1962. It is a long and complex document that treats issues as divergent as ideal class sizes and the need for all members of the institution to live as a community. Colville didn't anticipate that there would be "a lot of opposition to [this document] among the faculty." "By the spring of '61," he recalls with some regret in the interview, "after all the struggle to get this thing going, I was pretty discouraged. All of this made it almost obligatory that I get out of [this job]." Colville means that it was *emotionally* necessary for him to leave: he wasn't forced out. He is a dedicated person who always works hard toward a goal. But if his effort isn't showing the results that he expects, he will unilaterally withdraw. This reaction — which he's shown in other situations, such as his membership in the Legion and with his art dealers — isn't pique or sour grapes but the response of a decisive and independent person who channels his energies carefully.

Did Colville leave Mount Allison because he wanted to devote more time to his art? Certainly this was an important factor, yet he benefitted greatly from his teaching and struggled with the idea of giving it up. His interest in art history figured prominently in both his pleasure in teaching and, paradoxically, in his decision to abandon it. Colville remembers that he kept saying to Harris, "We should have a real art historian here," someone with a PhD. He got his way in 1961, when Helen Dow (who later wrote the first monograph on Colville) was hired. Her arrival meant, however, that she taught the art history class from which Colville was gaining so much. "This was another reason why I quit," he muses in the interview, "because the thing I enjoyed most was teaching art history."

A further reason why Colville resigned was that he was becoming more successful as an artist. He'd had his first solo exhibition outside Canada in New York in 1953. Yet he was not making much money from his art, and he really couldn't afford to quit his job. In the interview, he recalls the circumstances of his resolution to leave Mount Allison: returning from New York in February 1963 after his first show at the new Banfer Gallery, he went for a walk with Rhoda and decided "that I was going to quit my university job . . . effective June '63." No doubt he felt some confidence because the Banfer Gallery had recognized what his art was about. As its promotional material put it, "The gallery has a definite point of view. It will dedicate itself to the support and promotion of the contemporary realist painters and painting, encouraging new talent headed in that direction." Yet Colville's decision was dangerous financially, and he recalls that his mother — from whom he claims to have inherited his business acumen — wasn't pleased when she heard the news. Colville anticipated risks, and he was right: "I then had a kind of hair-raising time for the next two years or so," is how he puts it now.

The year was a watershed for Colville: he resigned from Mount Allison and had no income, his mother died in August, and his relationship with the Banfer Gallery fell apart after Richard Bannet died, so he didn't have a dealer to sell his work. For the first time, he was a completely independent artist. In retrospect a harbinger of successes to come, in the autumn of 1963 he won the $5,000 Dunn International Award for *Dog, Boy and St. John River* (1958; the boy is based on Graham Colville) in an exhibition at the Beaverbrook Art Gallery in Fredericton.

Colville remembers how lucky he felt to receive the money at such a lean time (and how he resented paying income tax on the award!). But the Colvilles were still hard up. Around this time, Bruce records, Colville had to sell his life insurance to pay the bills.

SUCCESS AND INSECURITY

To his surprise, Colville's "productivity didn't significantly increase" when he was free of university duties. He now understands that, for him at least, "it's as if one has only so much to produce." The "emergences" from his unconscious that he believes shape his ideas and work happen only at fixed intervals, he says in the interview. And Colville wasn't selling much of what he did make. Despite the welcome infusion of "$9,000 to $12,000" from his commission in 1965 to design the coins for Canada's centennial, plus the amount from the purchase by the National Gallery of Canada in 1966 of his famous *To Prince Edward Island* (1965), Colville still needed money to support his family. The mid-sixties saw his national and international reputation rise dramatically: he represented Canada at the prestigious Venice Biennale exhibition in 1966; in the following year, he became an Officer of the Order of Canada (see Fig. 27; he became a Companion of the Order of Canada in 1982) and received an honorary doctorate from Trent University in Peterborough, the first of many such recognitions (see Fig. 10). Yet it wasn't until his exhibitions in Germany and England, and his connection with Marlborough Fine Art in London in the late '60s ("the General Motors of the art-dealing world," as he puts it in Bruce's article), that he was secure. For Colville, financial independence is perhaps the main measure of his achievement: "At the age of fifty, in 1970, I was for the first time more or less a success," he says in the interview.

In part, financial insecurity before 1970 led him to accept an offer to be a visiting artist at the University of California, Santa

Cruz, in 1967–68. His affiliation with university life and teaching wasn't over. "I knew by the spring of '67 that we were going to go to Santa Cruz," he says. The salary was $20,000 American, or about three times what he had received latterly at Mount Allison. Money was the main reason for the move, though he was also pulled by the idealistic aspirations of this new university. He has always preferred to work in his home environment, and because 1967 was the first year at Dalhousie University in Halifax for the Colvilles' daughter, Ann, he didn't want to leave Sackville. Although Ann did well, Colville now "regret[s] very much that we went to California . . . in her first year. . . . [It's] something I would never do again," he says. He also had mixed feelings about California. "I felt something about California," he admits in Bruce's article, and ". . . I might have considered living in California. In some ways, it's very advanced . . . a mixture maybe of the best and the worst things the future has in store for us." He had been impressed with John F. Kennedy, and he was distressed at the dissolution, throughout the mid-sixties, of political hope in the United States. On the other hand, he enjoyed Santa Cruz and his colleagues. He was asked to stay on, but "At the end of the year," he notes in "The World," "although I liked the place and needed the money, we decided to go home. So I said, 'I want to go home,' like a child in a way." Colville's closest associate at Santa Cruz, an English-born biologist named Kenneth Thiman who was provost at the college where Colville worked, responded, "I wish you'd stay. What is it you don't like? I don't understand why you are so anxious to go back home." Colville explained his homing instinct this way: " 'you are a citizen of the world — I am a provincial. . . . My wife and I are both kind of rubes. . . .' And that is part of being Canadian, I think. An American . . . takes the United States with him," but a Canadian does not do likewise. So the Colvilles returned to Canada in June 1968. A few years later, Colville was urged by Harry Fischer to relocate to London, England, but he wouldn't leave Canada. "I wouldn't give up my Canadian citizenship for anything in the world," he asserts in Stewart's article.

Colville's rootedness in Atlantic Canada — and specifically in a few locales within this region[8] — is a salient feature of his nature. Although he celebrates the natural beauty of this area, it is not his prime reason for staying there. In Stewart's article, he jokingly says that after the war, "I . . . took a perverse satisfaction in living in an area which in a sense was 'nowhere.'" Colville wants and needs to belong in a place, to know and be a part of what's going on there. In this sense, he is a "provincial" and "rube," but in his case these terms do not carry their usual connotation of a lack of sophistication. Significantly, as he notes in the interview, the Colvilles carried two reminders of home with them to Santa Cruz: an old clock that now stands on their living room mantelpiece in Wolfville, and a sewing table that had belonged to Colville's late mother. Clearly the table has sentimental value, perhaps because it is reminiscent of his mother's sewing, which she began in Toronto and continued in the dress shop that she managed in Amherst, Nova Scotia until her death in 1963. We see this table in the foreground in *Pacific* (1967; Fig. 5), a troubling image that Colville began in the fall of 1967 in Santa Cruz and finished there. The figure is based on the artist, whose back faces us as he looks out at the ocean. Behind him, on the table, is a semiautomatic weapon (the Browning pistol that Colville had carried in the war, Burnett points out [206]). The image suggests that the man is contemplating murder or suicide. Colville sees it as an image of the dichotomies of life, "purity and eternity" in the ocean versus the "nasty business of actual life" represented by the gun (206). The immediacy of this juxtaposition strikes us when we realize that the weapon lies on a table dear to the artist. Keeping these elements in play, we look at an image of potential violence, of Colville's subconscious sensing of the disquiet then peaking in American society. Martin Luther King was assassinated in March 1968, around the time that Colville had received the invitation to stay in California. Robert Kennedy — brother of J.F.K. and president apparent —

was murdered in June. Characteristically knowing his mind, Colville withdrew from this troubling environment. Bruce notes that the Colvilles returned home the day after Robert Kennedy's assassination.

A less dramatic but equally important factor keeps Colville working at home. He likes to be independent and will do surprising things to maintain his freedom. A small incident illustrates this point. In the mid-sixties — he doesn't recall the date — Colville received a letter from the prestigious Guggenheim Foundation in New York "virtually inviting me to submit an application for a Guggenheim" Fellowship. These awards are offered to a small number of scholars and artists each year and are perhaps the most distinguished fellowships in the English-speaking world. Colville says in the interview that he "thought about" applying: "it came at a time when I was really short of money, . . . [but] I decided I didn't want to do it." Why not? He finds it difficult to articulate his reasoning but says, revealingly, "I would actually find [the fellowship] inhibiting. . . . I would be thinking, I've got this grant for this year, 'X' number of thousand dollars," and I have to do something specific to fulfil my responsibilities. He knows that he is most creative in a familiar setting, when he doesn't force his ideas. He obeyed the same instinct when offered another notable award in 1971, the opportunity to work in Berlin. This offer was, like that from Santa Cruz, to work abroad for one year; Colville, however, negotiated an unusual six-month term because he didn't want to be away from his studio for too long. Asked if he would accept a similar position today, he says that he doesn't think so. For the same reasons, Burnett notes, he is also wary about accepting commissions for his work (55). Colville is a creature of habit, and habit has served him well. Professor H.Y. Shih, former director of the National Gallery of Canada, and subsequently head of Fine Arts at the University of Hong Kong, said to him in 1985 "that she thought that I worked the way a dog chewed a bone." Colville the dog-lover is flattered; as he says in the interview, "I thought this was a very apt description. [My work is] very consistent, and it's very persistent, . . . [just as] a dog chews a bone in the same way one bone after another."

Recently Colville has found ways to maintain his contact with teaching and academia without compromising his need to be in his studio. In 1973, the family moved to Rhoda's familial home in Wolfville, and Colville turned the third floor into a studio and office. Although he doesn't have much contact with the humanities departments at Acadia, Colville was its chancellor from 1981 to 1991. He enjoyed his official role, and Godard notes that he was successful as a fundraiser for the university. For a month in 1985, he was a visiting artist at the University of Hong Kong. Such appointments and invitations result from Colville's fame and integrity. Godard, who has known him since the early 1960s, explained in an interview on 15 December 1992 that his is a "voice of rectitude; [one knows that] he can't be bought." As we see in *The Sweetest Spring*, he is comfortable and effective as a diplomat.

How *does* Alex Colville perceive himself now? His answer is typically disarming: "I think of myself — and I know this sounds vain — but I think of myself as a sort of self-appointed aristocrat." He has that bearing and charm, perhaps even a touch of noblesse oblige. He is not falsely modest, though sometimes he's self-deprecating. "The last time we were in Amsterdam," Colville recalls with some pleasure in the interview, "I said to Rhoda, 'I've made reservations at the Amstel Hotel, because when I was there after the second war, the only people who could stay in the Amstel Hotel were lieutenant colonels and above." Colville has worked for the success that he now enjoys; he appreciates life because he recognizes its fragility and evanescence.

THE FRAGILITY AND AFFIRMATION OF LIFE

Alex Colville is confident and decisive, someone who knows and speaks his mind. For many, these are appealing qualities, those of a leader, and he has considerable visibility and authority in Canada. His certitude about his values and priorities comes primarily from his ability to keep an honest perspective on himself and the world, to deal with both the good and bad in life. This strong sense of self makes him approachable, yet he has a certain aura, a formality and distance. David Burnett has seen the combination of awe and respect that Colville commands even in Wolfville, where he is well-known: "people will approach him, yet there's a sense that he's six inches taller" than everyone else, he says in a personal interview. Paradoxically his strength of character comes from his awareness of life's fragility. From what he calls his deep "sense of contingency" in *The Sweetest Spring* — what the novelist Joseph Conrad (one of Colville's favourite sources) pictured as the thin shell of civilization around chaos — arises his resolve to affirm what is stable and healthy in the world. This "enhanced consciousness of the fleetingness of life," as Hans Werner puts it, has led Colville to stress mortality at a convocation address (when everyone expected a speech about their bright futures), and to intimate the constant propinquity of violence in *Pacific* (Fig. 5) and other works. "I do have a fear of chaos," he confesses in Mays's article, "and a strong sense of the fragility of civilization. . . . I have contempt for apolitical people. If people take [civilization] for granted, it all falls apart."

At the same time, his own life is harmonious by design, and he produces images, such as *Moon and Cow* (1963; Fig. 12), whose technical purity underscores the perfection of their themes. About this work, Colville says in *Diary*, ". . . I suppose people think of cows as being stupid in their calmness. To me this seems like a virtue you see, this kind of serenity, tranquility which I associate with cows and in a way with the moon too, [and] it seems an important kind of virtue to me." Yet even in this harmonious image, we are left with a shard of doubt. The animal can't see the symmetry or feel the serenity; we supply these "virtues" and strive to maintain them, but we're always in danger of losing such orderliness. Even as a tremendously successful artist, Colville has a nagging "sense of the possibility of failure . . . [in his work], whether conceptual or technical." Paradoxically, then, "on a certain level, he appears relaxed and in

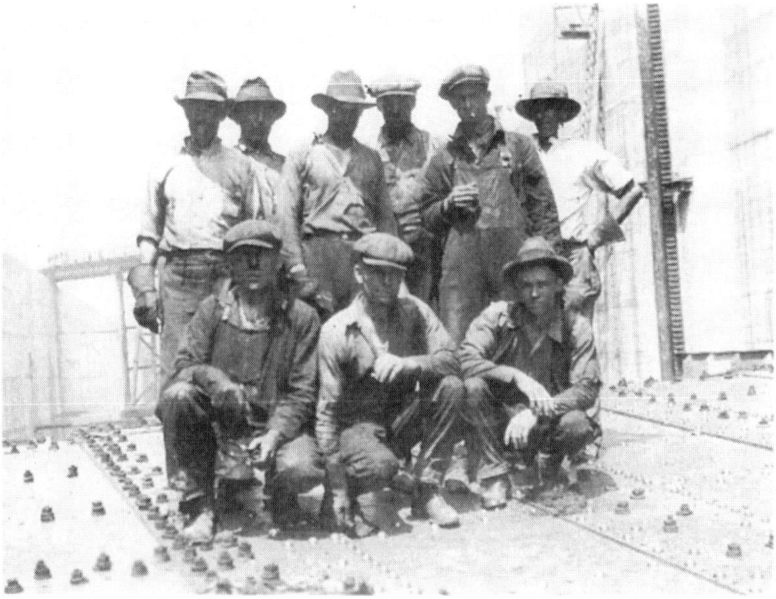

FIGURE 9

Colville's father, near St. Catharines, Ontario, 1928 (standing, at right): he was foreman of a riveting crew on Welland Canal.

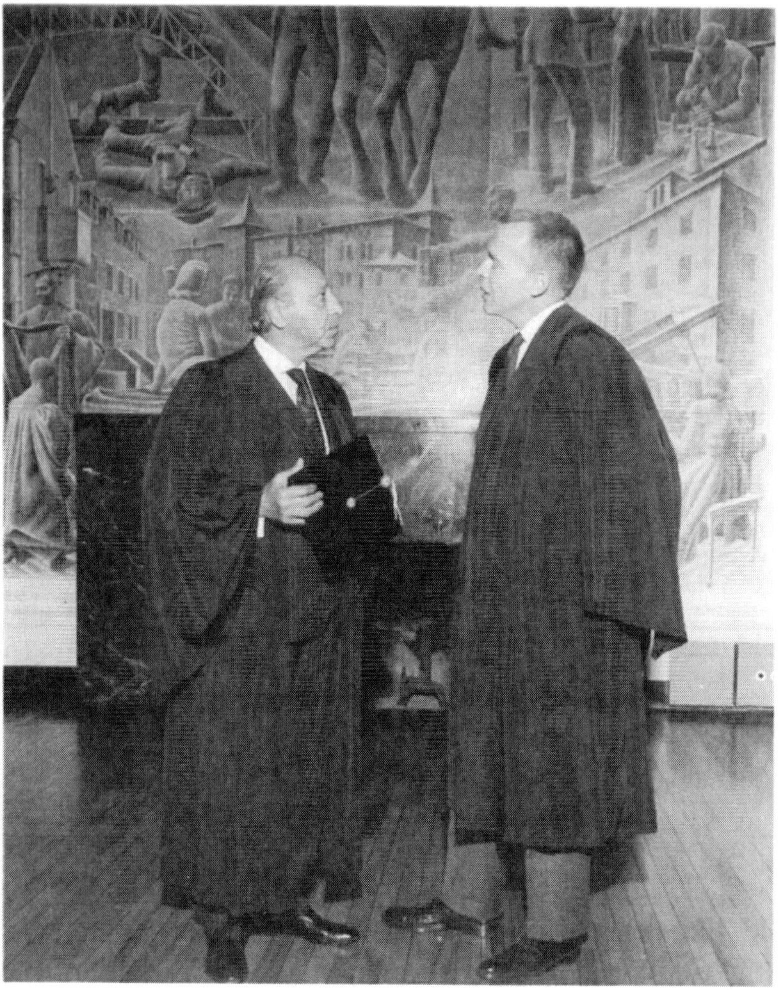

FIGURE 10

Colville with Canadian photographer Yousuf Karsh, 1968: occasion is their receiving honorary degrees from Mount Allison University, Sackville, New Brunswick. Colville's mural The History of Mount Allison *(1948) is in background.*

control of things, yet he'll say that there is always anxiety in coming up with new work," Burnett points out in a personal interview. For this reason, Colville's art is certainly not an escape from the troubles of life, however idyllic some of his images appear. It is an "appraisal of what life seems to be about," Colville says in his address. For him, life is about fragility and mystery. Sometimes it is menacing, but it also yields rare yet precious moments of "grace," "times," he says in Bruce's article, "when everything is okay." He solidifies these qualities in his art and tries to maintain a balance between their positive and negative implications. "Life," he speculates in *Diary*, "is characterised by its lack of permanence. Art, I think, tries to compensate for this. Art tries to be permanent, tries to extract from the transitory, that which is durably meaningful."

Colville's sense that life is fragile, that it both deserves and requires reaffirmation in his daily routine and work, stems from his background. Many people of his generation (he was born in 1920) are careful with money, seeing it as a measure of success, because they lived through the Depression. Colville's father managed to keep his job as a steelworker and riveting foreman through the 1930s (see Fig. 9), but his salary was cut in half when the effects of the stock-market crash of September 1929 hit the Nova Scotia economy with full force in the early 1930s. Many who fought in World War II have a special keenness about the value and evanescence of life. And many who have witnessed the social upheaval of the 1960s — and the apparent falling-off of political idealism since then — feel apprehensive about their society. Colville shares these experiences and some of these reactions, but as we have seen, specific aspects of his past figure in his worldview.

ILLNESS

Although Colville reports at seventy-two, in the interview, that he has been "an extraordinarily healthy person," two bouts with life-threatening illnesses have given him a special sense of life's delicacy. In 1989, he was hospitalized "for the first time in [his] life" for a hernia, he writes in a letter dated 15 January 1992, which in turn "led to prostate trouble," as he puts it, "and by good luck they found some cancer; I say '*good* luck' because I was sent [from Halifax] to [the] Johns Hopkins [University Hospital in Baltimore] and operated on by a famous surgeon." Dr. Patrick Walsh had "invented a new operation for prostate cancer which does not have the bad effects of earlier versions of this operation. So I am completely well." Colville's good fortune didn't end with the discovery of the cancer. He was also lucky that Walsh — an internationally renowned surgeon who couldn't possibly treat all those who needed his expertise — decided to take his case. Walsh wouldn't operate on anyone over seventy; Colville was sixty-nine in the summer of 1989 when he went to Baltimore.

Naturally he worried about the disease and its treatment and even reflected on mortality generally. In *The Sweetest Spring*, he tells his thirteen-year-old granddaughter that the "prospect of dying [is] not absurdly inappropriate in [one's] late sixties." Certainly he had thought about dying in the war, but it is hard to see in perspective in one's twenties, the age at which most of the soldiers whose graves the Colvilles visited in the Netherlands died. His brush with cancer brought those feelings back with great immediacy. Colville had also thought about death when he was only a few years younger than Ann. His 1980 recollection in "Alex Colville on Alex Colville" of an affliction with pneumonia captures his feelings well:

> When I was nine, only months after we had moved to Amherst, I got pneumonia. I was delirious for many days and in fact I nearly died. Convalescence was very long and I was in bed for several months. I stress this . . . because I think it had an effect on me. . . . I was lifted out of association with my friends and schoolmates. All through that spring and summer [of 1929] I led an almost solitary life. In this period I became what we usually call an introvert, one whose life is essentially a kind of inner life. I began to read,

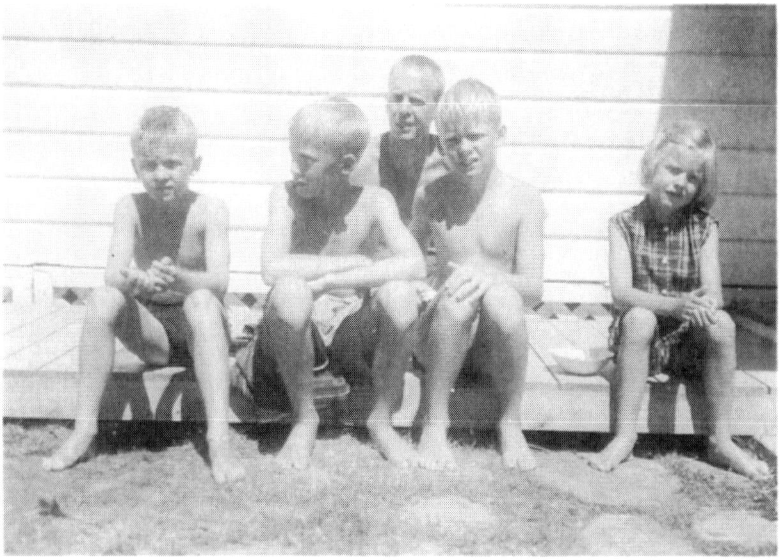

FIGURE 11

Colville (third from left) with his children, around 1955: left to right are Charles, Graham, John, and Ann.

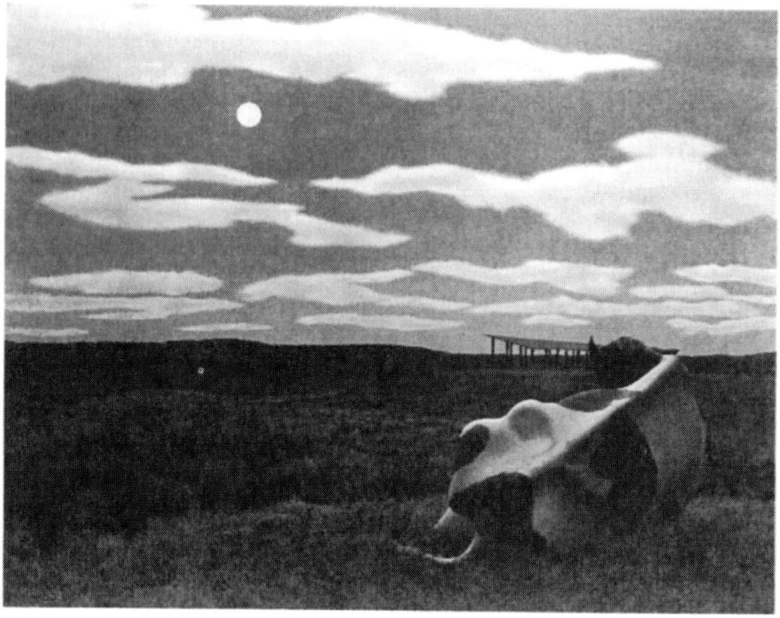

FIGURE 12

Colville, Moon and Cow *(1963): oil and synthetic resin, 68.5 x 91.4 cm., private collection.*

> really for the first time, and I did quite a few drawings, simply because I was alone and had to find something to do.

Not only his remarkable responsiveness to the goodness of "ordinary" occurrences, but also his initial interest in, and daily reaffirmation of, art, can partly be traced to his confrontations with mortality: his childhood pneumonia, the war, and prostate cancer.

World War II affected Colville even before he joined the army. He began university in 1938. By 1939, the hostilities had started, and, as he writes in "Alex Colville on Alex Colville," "by the time I was a third year student the real war was on. The Germans had overrun virtually the whole of the European continent and from that time on, the war was something one thought about. It affected student life, made it more sombre." During the war, Colville saw his share of destruction and human suffering. Then there was Belsen, which left a lasting image of civilization's capacity for cruelty and evil. And day to day he was painfully aware of his separation from Rhoda and then Graham, the son whom he didn't meet until returning to Canada in 1945. Although he felt accepted in the army as an artist — perhaps more than in civilian society — Colville felt uprooted by being away from home for so long. Perhaps more than seeing the termination of life, being displaced made him cherish everyday realities. We see this in the subject of his war art (see Fig. 7) and subsequent art.

True to his philosophical nature, Colville has theorized the importance of belonging in a place and culture. Referring to an article by Robert Fulford on the Toronto psychiatrist Vivian Rakoff,[9] he says in "The World,"

> One of Rakoff's special interests is that he thinks . . . that if you move too much you go crazy. He has made a study of the problem of immigration, of the trauma that the immigrant experiences. My father was an immigrant and I know that he had in many ways a very difficult life and that he experienced terrible uprootedness. Every time you move,

you lose your friends, you lose your known environment, you undergo what is in a certain sense a real trauma. . . . I like being where I know what is going on.

Colville's father emigrated from Scotland to Canada in 1910, and the family moved several times over the next twenty years as his jobs changed or shifted location. Alex Colville dislikes this sort of disruption, conceivably because he felt its consequences while growing up and, as Burnett points out, saw his father's life as one of professional disappointment (140). His art compensates for or counteracts both the sense of an immigrant's displacement and lack of professional opportunity with an emphasis on the familiar and stable, and his life imitates the regularity and precision of his art. Some people find Colville's compulsion for personal regularity amusing. For him, however, it makes work possible and affirms what is most real in life — it both recognizes and immunizes against mortality.

Colville manifests his need for security — for knowing what's going on — more tellingly than most people. His self-image as a banker and aristocrat is certainly different from the usual persona adopted by — or forced upon — those who are truly "starving artists." His search for a lifestyle and art safe from contingencies stems from his cognizance that they are inevitable. He affirms life by living it well materially and emphasizing its goodness pictorially. Certainty and security are for Colville thus compensatory values, ones that he needs to reestablish as constantly as he reexperiences their opposite, the fragility of our lives.

The topic of money often comes up in Colville's conversation. He doesn't brag, but he is pleased that he has "actually done well in worldly terms," as he puts it in the interview. In 1982, for example, he earned about $200,000 from the sale of paintings and prints — but paid nearly half of it in tax. He is more aristocratic than ostentatious in his personal habits. He just likes the best. When he was younger (and less successful), he had "the kind of attitude of an infantry lieutenant, that you don't eat better food than your men have, and you don't get any more sleep." But he's changed his mind about how to keep his morale high, a rare case, he recognizes, "where I've changed from one set of values to another." Colville now behaves as a colonel (or diplomat, or aristocrat) and stays at the Amstel Hotel. His new attitude is not so much symptomatic of his enjoyment of the good life — though it is partly that — as it is of his achievement of status in Canadian society. From his war days on, Colville has rubbed shoulders with people of high rank. He reports that J.A. (Alex) Corry, former principal at Queen's University in Kingston, a close friend with whom Colville served on The Canada Council from 1966–72 and whom he greatly admired, showed him that travelling first class is his privilege at his level of accomplishment. Colville disregards the response that artists shouldn't act this way because they're different. On the contrary, he argues, "I think this [way of living] is getting artists out of this idea of being slaves" in society. His is a hierarchical society, and he feels that he has earned the right to be at the top.

What he calls "entrepreneurial skill" and a self-proclaimed conservatism have brought him to this relative security. He claims that his business sense was a genetic gift from his mother, which manifested itself when he was twelve. At this time, Colville made drawings and then scale models of airplanes. "I used to sell them as soon as I got bored with them," he says in "Alex Colville on Alex Colville." "My early instinct to sell things began then. . . . Once I had done it, I didn't want to see it anymore." Perhaps he's grown more sentimental about his work: in the Colville's home hang several artist's proofs of serigraphs, including *Raven* (1990), which hangs above the mantelpiece in their living room. Yet Colville has little trouble "letting go" of works: "when he's satisfied with a piece, then that's the best it can be," Burnett notes in a personal interview. Colville was moved by his 1983 retrospective, Burnett also says, not because he was worried about the quality or reception of works that he had not seen for so long, but because they were like family members not thought of for years, then rediscovered.

ART DEALERS

A look at Colville's relations with art dealers shows how central money matters have been to him. If his business acumen comes from his mother, then "the romantic stuff," not to be undersold in his makeup, "comes from [his] father," he says in the personal interview. Reflecting on his international success — from the Venice Biennale in 1966 to the segment of his 1983 retrospective that was shown in Hong Kong, Beijing, Tokyo, and London in 1984–85 (see Fig. 13) — Colville acknowledges in one breath both impulses in his character: "I would still like to have an international presence," the wistful romantic says, "which I no longer have." But "basically, as long as I'm making a living, I don't care where the money is coming from." In other words, Colville would like to sell work in France or Germany, as in the past, but a sale in Nova Scotia (the first of which he had recently) pays the bills just as well. The money, and the sense of making a living from art, seem more important to Colville than ephemeral international acclaim.

Indeed, financial concerns have been central in Colville's relationships with art dealers. Pleased in the early 1950s with his work's ability to convey a certain mystery — as we see, for example, in *Nude and Dummy* (1950; Fig. 14) — Colville went to New York for the first time in May 1952. He was interested in sales more than the romance or glory of the world's art capital. He recalls that he went to several dealers with photographs of recent work. The Downtown Gallery was an early stop because it handled the work of Ben Shahn, a contemporary American painter whose work Colville still admires. The proprietor thought that the young Canadian might want to meet Shahn. He "reached for the phone and said 'Would you like to meet Shahn?' and I said 'No, no,' " Colville recalls in the personal interview. This was a business trip. Realizing this, the proprietor suggested that Colville see Edwin Hewitt, another gallery owner in New York. "Somewhat to my amazement," Colville reflects, "Hewitt said that he was interested in my work. . . . [He] was my first

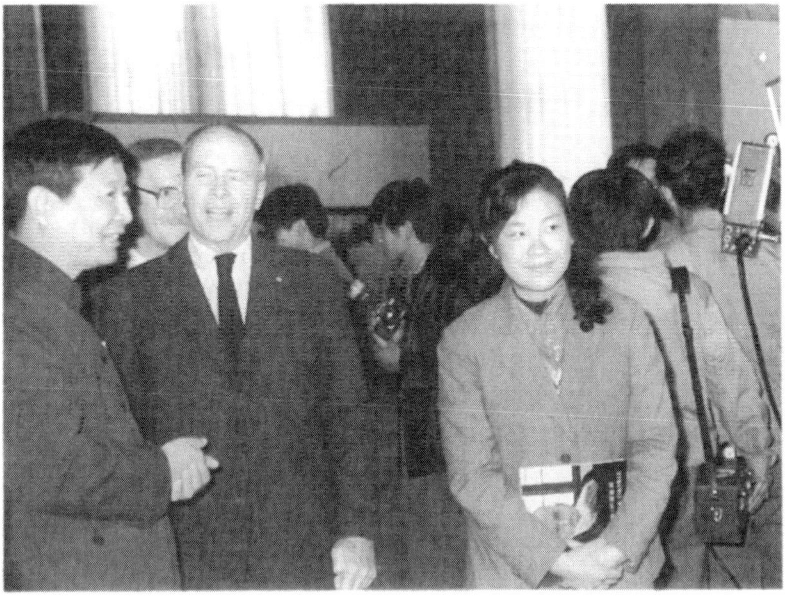

FIGURE 13

Colville at his exhibition opening in Beijing, December 1984: one of four international stops arranged by the Department of External Affairs in 1984–85.

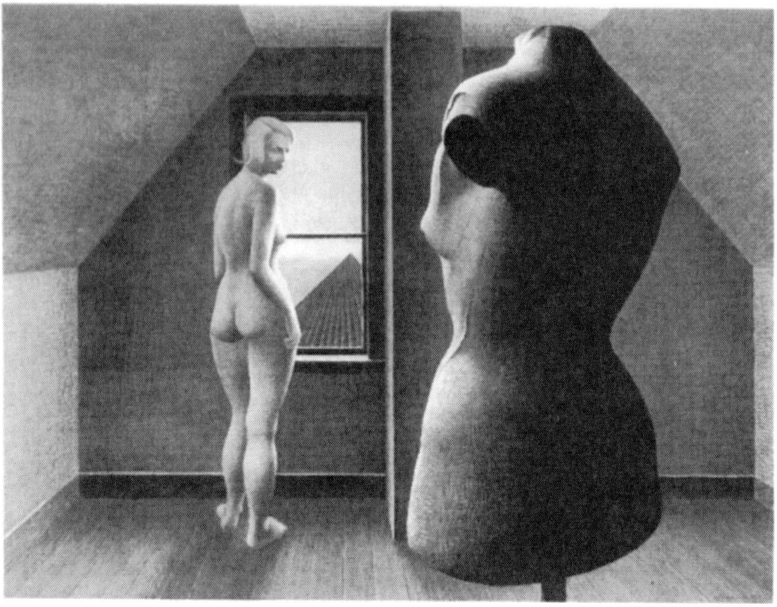

FIGURE 14

Colville, Nude and Dummy *(1950): glazed gum arabic emulsion, 60.9 x 81.2 cm., collection of New Brunswick Museum.*

dealer, and I had two exhibitions [at the Hewitt Gallery], one in '53 and one in '55." His exhibitions were "successful," with several works being sold, but Hewitt left to live in Japan in 1955 and closed his gallery. Habitually feeling that he needs a personal relationship with a dealer, Colville left the Hewitt Gallery and looked for someone else to handle his work.

The next episode in this history reveals Colville's sense of worth, good timing, and his willingness to hang tough to gain financial advantage. After leaving the Hewitt Gallery, Colville sent five paintings to the Dominion Gallery in Montreal, asking $300–$400 each, the going rate at the time. "A few days later," he recalls in Bruce's article, "I got a cheque from the man. He wanted all five paintings and the cheque was for $1,300. Just a little bit less. And I owed, I think, about $1,200. Well, I thought about it. Then I returned the cheque. I think I caught on relatively early. I've tried to maintain my independence." Colville repeats this story today with pride. After a brief and unprofitable connection with Laing Galleries in Toronto in 1958, he tried New York again, responding to an inquiry from Richard Bannet, who, with Tom Ferdinand, was starting up the Banfer Gallery and wanted to show Colville's work. They had seen an illustration of *Elm Tree at Horton Landing* (1956) on the front page of the *New York Times Book Review*. This association led to an important exhibition in the winter of 1963. Shortly after, though, Bannet died of a heart attack. Colville didn't want to continue with Ferdinand, and even "had some trouble getting him to return some [work,] . . . one of the rare times I've had any unpleasantness" with an art dealer, he says in the interview.

THE VENICE BIENNALE, 1966

The opportunity to represent Canada in the 1966 Venice Biennale — a premier international art show — led to Colville's association with the illustrious Marlborough Fine Art Gallery, with branches in New York and London. Dr. Harry Fischer, cofounder of Marlborough, and his son Wolfgang toured the Biennale separately and agreed that Colville's work stood out. Colville explains in the interview that "Harry, through Jean Boggs [at the National Gallery of Canada], got my address, and I sent things to [him] in the summer of '67," just before leaving for the visiting year in Santa Cruz. Fischer was instrumental in getting Colville exhibits and buyers throughout Europe, especially in Germany. The invitation for Colville to be a visiting artist in Berlin in 1971 can also be traced to Harry Fischer's efforts and the visibility that Colville's work had achieved.

In this year, Harry Fischer had a falling-out with others at Marlborough, and in 1972 thus formed Fischer Fine Art with his son in London. Colville was represented by this gallery until 1985. His daughter Ann worked for the Fischers for a time, and his relationship with the gallery was close. In retrospect, however, he thinks that he stayed with the Fischers too long, because Wolfgang did not seem to work as hard for him as Harry had. He had other options, especially in Canada. As Colville relates in the interview, "all this while, Mira Godard — beginning in '78 — had been very anxious to have me as part of her stable. She had an exhibition [of my work] in '78 through an arrangement with Fischer Fine Art." Godard — who had known Colville since he won the Dunn Prize at the Beaverbrook competition (and who celebrated thirty years in the art business in 1992 and remains one of the most respected dealers in Canada) — offered Colville representation at home and abroad. "Mira had been talking to Claude Bernard, a Paris dealer who also had a gallery in New York, and Mira and Claude and I met in London [England]." Their proposal was "that I would be represented by them jointly, and that some time in the reasonably near future, [I would have an exhibition] that opened in Paris, then [travelled] to New York and then to Mira's in Toronto." It was an ideal plan for Colville, but it failed, at least from his perspective. He claims that Bernard wanted an unreasonable number of works for the show — in effect asking Colville to quicken his pace. The three-stop exhibition, then, "was a dream that never materialized," though Colville's work was shown at Mira Godard in Toronto. Frustrated, he went to New York in early 1989 to have dinner with Bernard and talk things over. He quickly realized that "nothing seemed to be happening," and that "the whole thing [with Bernard] was just hopeless." As Colville tells the story, he severed his connection with Bernard on the spot, then phoned Godard to say that he wanted to see her. Over lunch, he "explained to her that this [breaking-off of their professional relationship] wasn't personal." Colville had entered the arrangement "based on the conception that Bernard would be part of it." Although he got on well with Godard and recognized that she was "disappointed," he was again — and as always, by his own choosing — without a dealer. Financial considerations were likely at the heart of his decision: Godard and Bernard couldn't meet his expectations for keeping his work visible and selling internationally. Godard reports in an interview on 15 December 1992 that the association wasn't working for them either. Bernard wanted to show Colville's work, and though he purchased several paintings himself, he couldn't get works quickly enough to mount a viable show.

Colville would still like to have the prominence afforded by international representation. For now, though, he seems happy to be associated with The Drabinsky Gallery in Toronto, owned by Garth Drabinsky and run by David and Marilyn Burnett. After leaving Godard's gallery in 1989, Colville was represented by Burnett, then a freelance dealer. Drabinsky opened his gallery in September 1990, and Colville's work was soon shown there. Legally, however, Burnett notes in the personal interview, Colville is still represented by David Burnett Associates. Godard suggests that Colville changed dealers partly to support Burnett, whose work for the 1983 retrospective he admired. Although Burnett doesn't describe their relationship this way, he admits that Colville generously supports people and causes that he finds worthy. Burnett claims further that such actions belie the image of Colville as aloof and austere, and, indeed, almost everyone who knows him describes him as warm and approachable —

anything but the "cold fish" of his own description and popular opinion.

ARISTOCRAT

Colville's preoccupation with money as a measure of success and guarantee of a certain order in life is connected to his avowed interest in power. A would-be aristocrat, he asserts in Perry's article that "I do not consider that I belong to the lower class; in fact, I have consciously and deliberately tried to move out of it. . . . I'm a person who's very interested in power," partly, he elaborates, because "The weak are defended by the strong. This is one of the reasons I am a conservative." Colville likes positions of authority in which he can do something positive, as we saw with his idealism in joining the Legion after World War II. He's also fascinated by abuses of power, both social and personal, and he depicts the need to address and control power in images such as *Target Pistol and Man* and *Pacific* (Figs. 4 and 5), in which the prominent pistols imply not only the power to commit suicide or murder, but also the power of control and accuracy (in the case of the target pistol). As Werner puts it, "The figure of justice, [Colville will] remind you, carries a sword in one hand. The use of power, he says, is a key moral and philosophical problem, and that's what his paintings featuring pistols are about. Power is a condition of life: a thing that must be handled."

If Colville has acquired sufficient power to take art out of its social position as a "slave" to other interests, at least for himself, we need to ask, first, how this assumption of authority relates to his perception of life's fragility, and second, how he has handled power. But first, what power does he have? Economic means and the resulting independence are major components, but his public stature is more significant because his voice is heard on major political and social issues of the day. And he has held several influential positions: president of the faculty association at Mount Allison, chancellor of Acadia University, two terms as a member of The Canada Council (1966–72), a member of the

Visiting Committee of the National Gallery in Ottawa, and latterly a board member there (1990–93). He has recently become a member of the Privy Council (1992). Colville has used these offices honestly to promote causes in which he believes. He is not power-hungry or authoritarian, yet his influence allows him to establish his version of order in the world.

For example, as a member of the National Gallery's search committee to replace Dr. Jean Sutherland Boggs as director, Colville worked hard to convince his fellow members to nominate Dr. Yen Shih, which they did. "She was basically a Chinese aristocrat," he recalls in the interview, and "I thought she was a very impressive person." His distaste for abstract art caused him to vote against the Gallery's proposed acquisition of American abstract expressionist Barnett Newman's *Voice of Fire* (1967) when he was on the Visiting Committee. He had made up his mind about *all* abstract art years before. "When I was forming as a young artist," he says in Mays's article, "I saw that the dominant movements were abstraction, expressionism and so on. I looked at it and said, so much for that." Colville "found [his] voice in 1950." No doubt he spoke passionately against the acquisition of this grand example of abstract painting, but he was in the minority, and the Newman was purchased to much controversy.

Newman's large canvas had hung in the American pavilion at Expo '67 in Montreal, a fact that did not endear it to the outspoken Colville. "I actually disapproved of Expo," he says in the interview, recalling a pre-Expo, CBC Television interview in which he claimed that the world's fair "was a terrible idea; I said I didn't think we had anything to celebrate and that it was just a foolish waste of money." Why? There are two reasons, one personal and one more reasoned: "I was against Trudeau, who I never had a high opinion of," and who seemed to be riding on the publicity for Expo. But Colville had also heard about the poverty in Montreal from a high-ranking federal civil servant, who had asked, "What are these people going to think when they see Expo?" Colville's comments to the CBC interviewer were too negative to be aired, but he held to his principles. "I simply refused to go to Expo," he says, and anyway "that was the year we were in California." As with the Newman painting, Colville's influence was not as great as he perhaps had hoped. Many people went to Expo. Canadian abstract art had a major presence there. Even his "great admiration" for former Nova Scotia Premier Robert Stanfield, then the Progressive Conservative's choice for prime minister in the next election, didn't help Canada in the late 1960s. "I thought when we went to California that without any question Robert Stanfield would be the next prime minister." Trudeau won a landslide victory.

WOMEN IN ART

Some people have accused Colville of abusing his power in the way that he depicts women in his paintings. Reviewing his large exhibition at The Drabinsky Gallery in 1991, for example, Shane Nakoneshny writes that Colville

> signif[ies] one vision of the world — that of the constitutive male subject. . . . [T]he women in his work (and some men) are often denied subjectivity, and their faces and hands are concealed. Moreover, other figures are . . . defined by gender-specific activities: e.g. women are portrayed at such relatively passive events as sunbathing (*Woman on Diving Board*), or playing musical instruments and singing (*Fête Champêtre, Singer*). . . .

She goes on to detail how men in Colville's work are active, often powerful figures. For Nakoneshny and others, Colville demonstrates an offensive objectification of women; he uses them as objects in his art. While many viewers see the threat of violence and the sadly unbalanced power relationship between men and women in images such as *Woman in Bathtub* (1973), Colville doesn't comprehend the criticism. He sees trust between husband and wife (Rhoda is often his model, as in this case). In a startling painting entitled *Woman with Revolver* (1987), we see a nude woman descending a staircase, revolver in hand. We can't see her face, only her body and the gun. Here Colville sees not *his* power in displaying the female nude but rather the "possibility of women being powerful creatures, which of course they are, I think," he says in his address. Do women have power because they carry handguns in their homes (at night, in the nude), or does this image suggest the unfortunate result of their powerlessness, their vulnerability to sexual violence? Colville agrees with the latter possibility to a certain extent, explaining that the idea for this image came partly from an episode of *Miami Vice* in which a female police officer shoots and kills a man who wields a knife. She uses a revolver with a two-inch barrel, Colville mentions in a letter dated 9 December 1992. He was also thinking of the famous Maoist saying, "Power comes out of the barrel of a gun." For Colville, then, the woman is threatened but not powerless.

He addresses these issues directly in *Western Star* (1985; Fig. 15). The image shows a woman, her back to us, being photographed by a man in overalls; a "Western Star" truck dominates the scene. To Colville, the man is "in awe of the woman," whom we take to be a celebrity, a "western star" herself. *Western Star* has become a particularly talked-about painting because it recently appeared on the cover of Acadia University's academic calendar and prompted several written complaints from women in the university community to the president. Their point was that the work shows contempt for women by making them objects, in this case, of the man's gaze and of photography. To these women, it is misogynistic and thus inappropriate on an official publication.

Colville's response to this incident? He didn't find out about it until months later, but he says in the interview, "I'm baffled. For someone to think of this as degradation just really shocks me. . . . It's not that I'm against feminism in general, but this aspect of it that came up with *Western Star* simply astonished me, and

I guess I would say that my feelings were hurt." He wanted to show in this picture that "women [are] mysterious, attractive." "I don't consider women . . . ordinary people": "It's not possible for any man to fully understand any woman," he says. He sees himself as trying to understand "what women want" without destroying the mystery of difference. Colville works and lives in this chivalrous, respectful, and ultimately hierarchical world as far as gender relations are concerned. When he constructs *Nude and Dummy* or *Western Star* (Figs. 14 and 15), or the many other images of women in his oeuvre, he affirms what is for him an ideal harmony. Yet many women and men would deny that his images embody the values that he wants to portray. Colville is uncharacteristically out of touch with much of "what's going on" in this sphere of human relations.

Whether we agree or disagree with what we see in Colville's images, it's important to recognize his commitment to "convey messages," to take on this moral responsibility, as he mentions in his address. This activity is another response to his perception of life's fragility and preciousness. He wrote in 1951, in "My Experience," that "painting should neither be fun nor primarily a means of self-expression. I regard paintings as things produced not to relieve the artist, not to serve him, but to serve other people who will look at them. . . ." Art, for him, is a matter of communication. He does not simply reaffirm his beliefs to himself in a loop of insecurity and vanity. He invites our engagement with his values: "the ability of the viewer to identify, to get into the thing," is crucial to him, he says in "The World"; and he's anything but dogmatic about which reactions are appropriate: "every individual brings to the examination of any given work of art a different experience, so that the work is different for everybody who looks at it." His tolerant standpoint doesn't imply that he lacks strong opinions on what particular works mean, or that his feelings can't be hurt by misinterpretation (as we've seen in the case of *Western Star*). In affirming what he sees as positive in life, however, he presents moral arguments. He shows us what he finds important, hoping for a response, and he

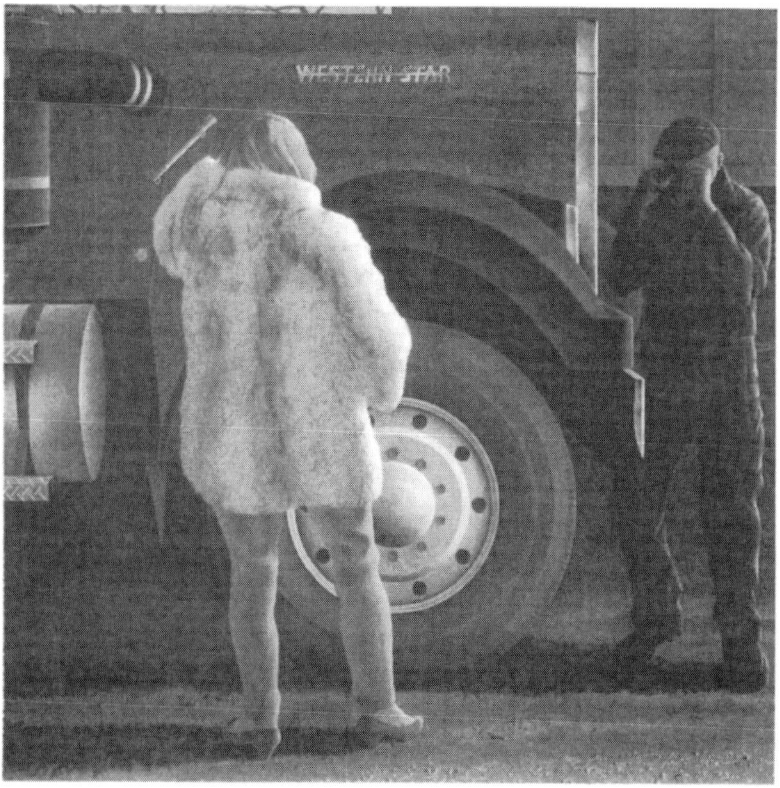

FIGURE 15

Colville, Western Star *(1985): acrylic on particle board, 73.8 x 73.8 cm., Lavalin Collection, Musée d'art contemporain de Montréal.*

won't let a work go until he feels that it's the best it can be. Burnett quotes him as saying more formally in 1981, when the artist's "attention to the continuous buzz and flicker of experience and his struggle to transmit these into forms results in an authentic work, other people will experience from it a kind of ordering, fulfilling, illuminating sensation" (18).

Whom does Colville seek to address? Most artists are primarily concerned to engage their peers, wanting currency and respect in this quarter. Colville aims at a more popular interaction and cares little about the judgements of the art world. "I have been struck for years by the hunger of people for images they can recognize," he claimed in 1983 in Mays's article. "They go to museums to see it, and [they] find abstract art is simply a bore. But my art is popular. People who do not normally look at art, look at my stuff." He knows that his works are recognizable and comprehensible, and thus different: "Perhaps the most remarkable feature of my paintings," Hammock quotes him as saying, "is that they are, to an extent unusual in art of this century, 'popular'; they do not belong exclusively to the art world. It may be argued that they do not belong to the art world at all." "Popular" is a positive description for Colville. It implies that "A taxi driver or an insurance salesman can come in and say 'that's a cow.' I don't think there is anything here that's arcane or out of the way," Eve Johnson quotes him as saying. For Colville, current popularity ensures the reputation that he and his work will have in posterity. He is able to voice his concerns in an admirably direct and popular way in Nancy Baele's article: "An artist will never be a star in the same way Anne Murray is a star. Millions of people will hear Anne Murray where my audience is limited to, at the very most, thousands."

Not surprisingly, Colville's unsolicitous attitude toward art experts has led to criticism of him and his work. Several well-argued commentaries take Colville to task for his views (for example, those of Nakoneshny and Perry), but the piece that stands out is an opportunistic, ad hominem attack that substitutes sensationalism for thinking. John Bentley Mays, reviewing

Colville's 1983 retrospective in the *Globe and Mail*, fumes in "Colville's Importance Exaggerated" that

> Whatever interesting things may be said of the eccentric, garrulous artist himself, the art he has made is of virtually no creative consequence. . . . Its widespread popularity and potential as a crowd-pleaser apart, Colville's art is worthy of inclusion in a small, didactic group show of realists from Canada's Atlantic region, nothing more.

Mays isn't one to pull punches, but he's also capable of insight. Why, then, is he so riled about Colville's successes? We sense that his popularity is the main reason: if something is celebrated, it just can't be good according to those in the know. It is decidedly uncool in Canadian art circles to appreciate Colville's work.

POPULARITY AND AUDIENCE

"I was annoyed at Mays [for] that thing he wrote when my exhibition opened in Toronto," Colville reflects in the interview. "Early on, I used to keep reviews, but I suppose it's decades since I have." Mays's review got to him: he'd let Mays interview him, and he and Rhoda were generous in their hospitality, only to be rewarded with a gratuitous denunciation. Burnett confirms in the personal interview that Colville was offended by "the man's lack of civility." Moreover, the exposure afforded by this critique in "Canada's National Newspaper" was important to Colville (Mays remains one of the most widely read art journalists in the country), and to suffer such a personal attack because of his popularity was galling. Colville says in the interview that "the whole art thing has become so specialized," and thus he wants to communicate his values beyond the often ingrown confines of the art world.

In addition to using accessible subject matter, Colville has other strategies that help him to reach a wide audience. He frequently allows his images to be used on book covers; there's a pile of such credits in his office. Those who envision him as a stuffy provincial will think again once they see the wonderful photo of him with rock singer Bruce Cockburn (Fig. 16), who used the famous *Horse and Train* (1954) on a record jacket. More directly, Colville has recently had several of his best-known images photographically reproduced to be sold for about $300 each, a fraction of the price for one of his *drawings*, let alone a serigraph or painting. "Some people are shocked that I've allowed these reproductions to be made," he exclaims in the interview, "but of course I've been wanting people to reproduce my paintings for decades." Burnett recalls in the interview that some of Colville's works were made into poster-quality reproductions in Victoria years ago, and that Colville "was quite pleased that they were done" if not with their quality. Hence, he has waited to try again, partly because the technology to make reproductions of the quality demanded by Colville the perfectionist has only recently become available. A greater barrier is the attitude that popular means bad. For example, he tried to convince Wolfgang Fischer of the viability of reproductions. "My stuff has popular appeal; reproductions will sell," he argued, but it didn't happen, as he points out in the interview. There is, of course, a financial incentive here in a new market for his work — a factor that Colville wouldn't scorn, especially given the crash of the art market in the '90s — but, for him, access to a wide audience remains paramount. Burnett quotes him as writing,

> But if one is not to accept the argument that my work is rather popular because it is bad (commercial, sentimental, retrogressive) then one is asserting that it is perhaps good, *although* popular. Then the question is: can this be possible? — and if it can be, how does one explain it? I am inclined to think that this is the central issue in considering my work. (17)

Popularity — or accessibility — *guarantees* affirmation of the values evident in Colville's work and life. If people looking from

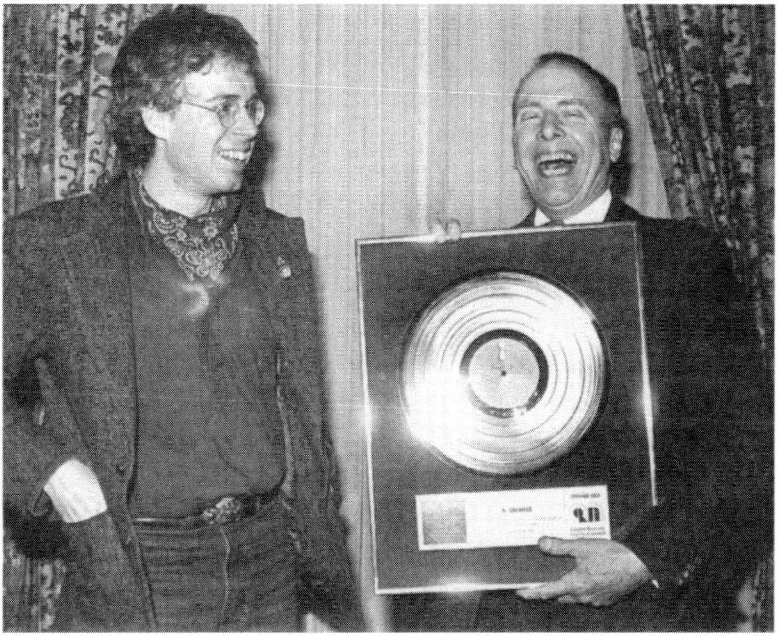

FIGURE 16

Colville with Canadian musician Bruce Cockburn, around 1976: Cockburn, who'd used Colville's Horse and Train *(1954) on a record jacket, presents him with a gold record.*

different perspectives and backgrounds see what he sees, then this recognition is a major factor in his championing of the popular. Is it also his earnest attempt to make his art approachable, to confer with others about what concerns him, that makes his work both good and popular? Many people think that much of contemporary art goes over their heads and is therefore condescending to the uninitiated. But Colville's work seems more honest, direct, and — paradoxically, given his views — that of a man of the people.

One aspect of his quest to address people frankly and on their terms is what he calls "authenticating" an image, that is, making it seem true to the experience of both viewer and artist. It may be surprising to those who praise the visual precision of Colville's finished works that he doesn't begin with a sharp image of what he wants to produce. He has inchoate, dreamlike, subconscious intimations and intuitions from which he works — through numerous drawings — to a finished picture. To get from the private and idiosyncratic to an image that is legible and meaningful to others, he works toward visual exactitude. As he says in the interview, "My beginning drawings for these things I do are always somewhat vague, semi-abstract, rough. At a certain point [though], I want to authenticate things, and for this, I either want to make quite specific, often measured drawings of whatever it is, and if that's not possible, I'll use photographs." We've seen the latter practice in the creation of *French Cross* (1988; Fig. 3). Colville's conviction that it is "very important to get the details right," as he says in his address, accords with common sense, and demonstrates that, for him, authenticating a work and addressing the popular are closely connected.

AUTHENTICITY AND CONTROL

Most of Colville's means for authenticating an image are technical: he measures objects (routinely carrying a measuring tape with him, Hammock notes), he plots their mathematical and geometric relationships to get the perspective right, and he seeks advice from experts on everything from technical specifications to the most durable papers to use in a print. In short, he gets to know the objects and situations that he portrays as intimately as he can. If the interior of the car in *Traveller* (Fig. 8) looks like that of a Porsche 911, then we can be sure that everything is as it is in the vehicle itself, even the safety inspection sticker in the left bottom corner of the windshield. If Colville portrays a Honda in *Kiss with Honda* (1989), to give a more accessible example, then we can be sure that it looks this way. The same is true in paintings without machines, such as *Dog and Groom* (1991), in which we see Colville and his dog in a bedroom of his home. Even the grain in the hardwood floor is exact. Like many Dutch and Flemish landscape and genre painters of the seventeenth century, he affirms what we see around us. We like to be shown the familiar because it is what we understand; it affirms our lives and values. Given the precision of Colville's finished work, we might be surprised to know that he often feels anxious that he won't have new ideas after a piece is finished, or that things won't go right during the painstaking process of authentication. For example, Burnett recalls in the interview that Colville "went crazy over *Köln Express* [1986] because he had great difficulty with the paper." The troublesome material was a heavy paper that he hadn't used before, and he had "real anxiety" that he wouldn't be able to succeed with the image.

If we extend the notion of authentication a little, it's clear that Colville's commitment to the craft aspects of his art is also a way to satisfy the conventional wishes of those who look at art on a popular level. We can see the work that he has done in the minute brushstrokes. He makes his own frames and produces his own silk screens (a tricky process that involves hazardous chemicals), and he crates his work before shipping it to his dealer. The precise yet complex spatial relations — and concomitant thematic puzzles — in Colville's works testify to his labour. He also wants his work to last. When he began using the newly available acrylic paints in 1963, Hammock writes, he sought the counsel of Ralph Mayer, an expert in New York, regarding their longevity. For his prints and photographic reproductions, moreover, he uses the best paper available.

We can see Colville's rigorous technical and cerebral control over the production of his images as a hedge against mortality, against what he knows is the inevitable passing of all things. Such metaphysical concerns resonate in his detailed description in *Diary* of his method of painting *Ocean Limited* (1962):

> . . . I've always been very much fascinated by the trains moving through this flat kind of country and I[,] at some mysterious point, . . . decide I'm going to do a painting of the [train called] Ocean Limited.
>
> Now I know that I'm going to build this up in a gradual way, building of course implies measurements, geometry; all builders use measurements and indeed most painters and sculptors of other ages have done this, so I start with a geometric scheme. . . .
>
> [T]he geometry of this particular painting is based on what is called a root three rectangle, and that's a rectangle in which the diagonal is exactly twice the shorter side. . . . So I plot this whole thing — the train, the man who is an important part of this painting and their relationship to the landscape. Then . . . I start in and I explore the elements of the general setup which will become the catch to this geometric bridge system. And I make drawings of the actual and specific part of the landscape, the railroad embankment, the poles, the grasses . . . , of the man, the person who is to be walking across here. This I had to do largely from memory, but I did make some drawings of a person with a raincoat and so on.
>
> Then I had to make very detailed drawings of the locomotive[,] which I wanted to be exact . . . , no artistic licence to speak of except in its placing. These things then are all fused in, synthesized back into this master geometric scheme. I then start the painting and it's very slowly built up with small brush strokes — a pale colour at first, gradu-

ally getting more and more clearly defined, it comes out of nothing, and ends I hope as something. It is a progression of nothing to something[,] which is a progression within this grid . . . [and] ends with things as clearly defined as I want them to be.

As I've suggested, these meticulous processes are more than technical: "I'm trying to make a painting that will not seem horribly inferior, [to] produce a world, make a world, that won't seem horribly inferior to the actual world that God has made . . . ," Colville further says.

COLVILLE'S IDEAL PUBLIC

It is notoriously difficult to define an artist's public, the group that responds favourably to his or her work. But if Colville's concern for the popular is a way of confirming to himself and others those aspects of life that are valuable yet precarious, we need to ask who does appreciate his work, and why. Or, if it's impossible to gather empirical data about this public, then perhaps we should ask about his *ideal* public, those with whom he hopes to communicate, and to whom he gives his vision of permanence. Clearly some people buy his original work, but given his low output and the high prices that he commands, they form but a small segment of his audience. Colville has mentioned taxi drivers and insurance salespeople, presumably because members of these groups — however diverse they may be as individuals — do not belong to the art intelligentsia. They will be "ordinary people," and for Colville, the "ordinary," in the sense of the everyday, is of the utmost importance. He suspects that what often troubles people about his work, in which they find mystery and intrigue, "may well be [in] the idea that ordinary things are important," he says in Johnson's article. A greater range of "ordinary" people have access to Colville's work than to that of any other living Canadian artist.

For example, thousands of copies of *Horse and Train* (1954) exist via the Cockburn record jacket (see Fig. 16). Millions of people have at least glanced at the centennial coins. Bannet and Ferdinand (of the Banfer Gallery in New York) noticed Colville's work because it adorned the jacket of a book that was reproduced in a newspaper review. His works hang in a number of Canadian and European public galleries, and he has painted two large murals at Mount Allison University (see Fig. 10). Journalists who are not primarily art critics write about Colville and his work (most prominent in this company is Robert Fulford). Mainstream art publications, such as *Canadian Art*, reproduce images of him and his paintings. Colville and his work are popular — by design. This happy situation evolved gradually, and it might seem to be a version of the proverbial chicken-and-egg problem: is Colville's work popular because it's so recognizable, or is it recognizable because it's so appealing? But his consistent philosophy has always had the potential to be communicated widely, and, in a sense, his works' popularity existed before it was extensively perceived. It also existed with his war art, well-received by the troops for whom it was made. Colville's views and methods haven't changed much in almost fifty years. His audience has simply grown larger and more diverse.

DETRACTORS

His status in Canada makes it incorrect to say that opinion is divided about him and his work: detractors, such as Mays, are in the minority. Two commentators in particular have focused on the implications of Colville's fame. The titles of the articles make their respective slants clear. In "Painter Laureate" — which appeared in July 1983 in *Saturday Night*, at the time that Colville's retrospective opened at the Art Gallery of Ontario in Toronto — Robert Fulford indirectly broaches the issue of what his popularity means. Colville, he claims, "has finally become our national painter and his art has become the visual embodiment of whatever is enduring in the Canadian imagination of this period." By contrast — in "Alex Colville: Why Have We Made Him Head Boy of Canadian Painters?" — Richard Perry takes issue with the habitually "soft" — that is, uncritical — response to Colville's work (Fulford's piece, for instance) in the general media and art press alike.

Perry sees Colville as "a painter who lacks spontaneity, improvisation, and subversiveness, and who extols discipline, structure, and 'elaborate systems of convention.' " Perry's real worry is that these "virtues" make Colville popular in Canada. In other words, he fears that Fulford is right when he claims that Colville and his work betoken Canadianness. Perry is too intellectually engaged in this article to launch an ad hominem attack, or to object — however indirectly — to an artist's work being popular. Both he and Fulford pose difficult, even embarrassing, questions about national identity. Fulford has no trouble with the notion that Colville is an icon of Canada; Perry finds the idea repulsive.

INTERNATIONAL ACCLAIM

Colville is fascinated by these issues, in particular how his popularity varies from one national group to the next. "One of the things that still puzzles me," he says in the interview, "is the unquestioned relationship between my work and German people. There's some kind of connection between my work and the German psyche." Colville's evidence for this affinity is the favourable response that his work has received in Germany. The most famous response to date was Heinz Ohff's 1971 contention that Colville is "the most important realist painter in the Western world." As further evidence, Colville cites ongoing requests to use his paintings on book jackets, and, more important if we think of his popularity, repeated requests to autograph postcards of *Truck Stop* (1966), which hangs in the Ludwig Museum in Köln (Cologne), Germany. He is aware of the irony of this situation, given his ambivalence about Germany at one time and the generally cool reception of his work in Great Britain. Yet the question of national types and proclivities seems genuine, though notoriously difficult to fathom.

Writing about one of Colville's most acclaimed earlier paintings, *To Prince Edward Island* (1965), purchased by the National Gallery of Canada, a British critic (whom Perry quotes) wrote in the prestigious *Burlington Magazine* that "What remains" for the viewer "is the impression of an idea that, because it is not related to any overall visual philosophy, strikes the eye like an affected gesture." If this negative sentiment is symptomatic of responses in England, then we can understand why no one there, according to Colville in the interview, has ever purchased one of his works. By contrast, he has sold frequently in Germany. Colville's tentative explanation is that his work is serious, that "the idea of seriousness is basically un-English" but quintessentially German. His former dealer, Wolfgang Fischer — Austrian by birth and thus part of German culture — provides a related rationale in "The World." Seeing the large collection of Colville's work at the retrospective that opened at the Art Gallery of Ontario in the summer of 1983, Fischer exclaimed to Colville: "You know, when I come in and see this great assemblage of your work, I realize why the Germans so like your work." It's because "This is German Romanticism" in the twentieth century. German Romanticism — represented especially by the early nineteenth-century artist Caspar David Friedrich — is characterized by the meticulous finish of the surface and, more significantly, the level of metaphysical implication that we also find in Colville's paintings. He has for years been drawn to Friedrich's work, and Ohff also compared the two in his 1971 review.

There is much meditation on death, on the evanescence and preciousness of life, in German Romantic painting. Lone or grouped figures are often depicted with their backs to us, pondering great mysteries such as the moon or ocean. This seriousness is stereotypically German in the arts, and it's characteristic of Colville's attitude, too. Such thoughtfulness, and his refusal to endorse such apparently forward-looking projects as Expo '67, have led some to see him as "a pessimist, a conservative who

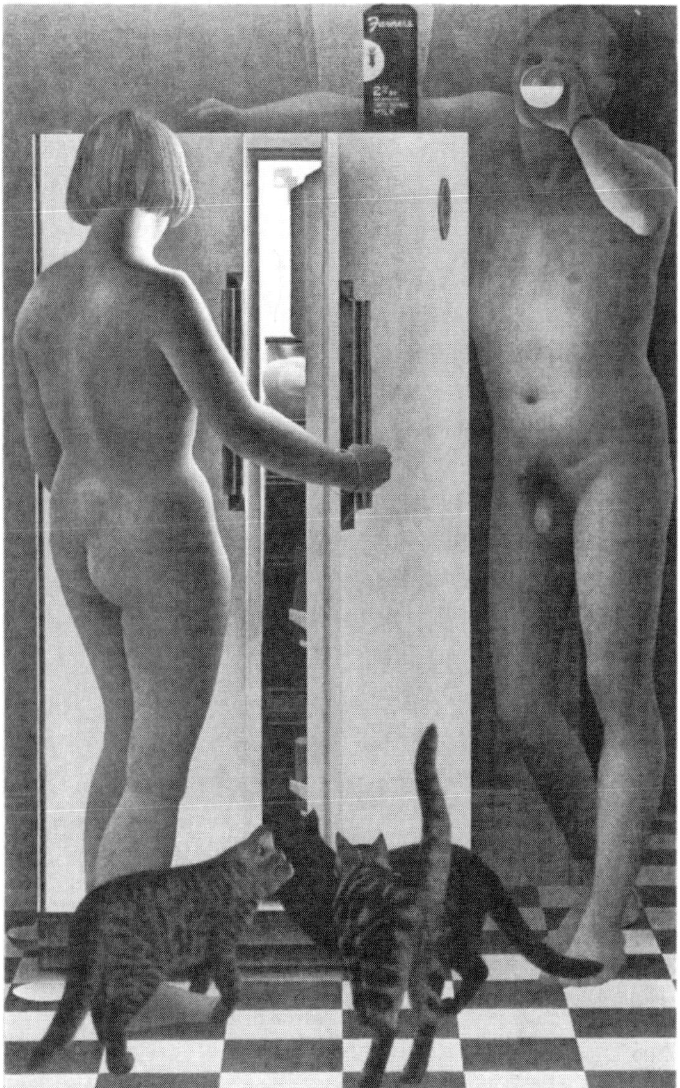

FIGURE 17

Colville, Refrigerator *(1977): acrylic polymer emulsion, 120 x 72.4 cm., private collection.*

regards modernity with suspicion and clings to the traditional values of his adopted region, the Maritimes," as Fulford has it. Colville counters this view by saying that being aware of mortality, of life's dangers — the concerns grouped here under the term "fragility" — is a realistic, not a pessimistic, stance. "I am an optimist in my everyday life," he claims in an article by Gilles Toupin. "But my views about human destiny are not cheerful. My work is pessimistic but my life is happy. I believe that the human condition is tragic" (my translation). He is proud of his personal and political conservatism, and he feels that his attitudes and values don't turn him into a pessimist. We've seen that he views disturbing images such as *Woman and Bath* or *Target Pistol and Man* (Fig. 4) as positive within his philosophy of life. Although he can't and wouldn't deny a viewer of his works negative responses, his sanguine attitudes about life are consistent with his feelings about his art. Fulford confuses Colville's caution about the world with pessimism. Even more glaringly, he ignores Colville's overtly positive affirmations of ideas and mores that transcend regional boundaries.

THE AFFIRMATION OF LIFE

Let's look at his affirmation of life by considering two paintings, *Refrigerator* (1977; Fig. 17) and *French Cross* (1988; Fig. 3). In the first we see a familiar scene, the nighttime visit to the refrigerator. For some viewers, this "familiarity" is taken too far, and Colville has been criticized for the nudity here (apparently they are more concerned with male than female nudity, an ancient tradition in art). In Colville's view, however, this is an image of domesticity. Typically he has used himself and Rhoda as models. His depiction is frank, but the emphasis is on the couple, on communal activity (even the cats'), not on their undressed state. They share the search for a midnight snack. In its harmony, then, this is an edenic scene: Colville even suggests in Toupin's article that he and Rhoda are Adam and Eve in the garden.

In addition to their sharing and the apparently wordless communication, it's also possible to read here another of Colville's views on life, one already discussed with respect to the woman in *Western Star*, that men can't completely know women and must rather stand in awe of them. The two figures are not entirely equal in *Refrigerator*, even though they share an activity. Colville has made his decision about food first. He is shown drinking his milk, a wonderful moment of authentication that also works to generalize the image by obscuring his facial features. Rhoda and the cats ponder the situation. Her intimacy with the artist is somatic. No glances are exchanged between the Colvilles, and we speculate that this is a well-known, nightly ritual, one in which Alex knows what he wants to drink and always has the same thing while Rhoda muses on the possibilities. In a way, then, it is an image of the ordinary, both in their lives and those of many people. The ordinary is important; it must be affirmed and becomes uncanny if we think about it for long enough, as this image invites us to do. On the other hand, the "immodesty" of the scene is fictive: in real life Rhoda wouldn't find herself in the kitchen unclothed. Perhaps, then, it is the fact that the unusual is made to seem ordinary or domestic that gives this picture its mysterious charge.

Refrigerator rehearses and valorizes a domestic experience; how this affirmation works in *French Cross* (Fig. 3) is less obvious — perhaps also more complex — and it reveals Colville's sense of history and morality. Like many of his works, *French Cross* is a conglomerate of ideas taken from different times and places. The cross, which stands at the Grand Pré, only a few kilometres from Wolfville, is a commemorative monument to the Acadian people forced to leave this area by the English in 1755. Colville had made drawings of this cross in 1983, but couldn't think of how to use them in a composition. "Then, I got this brainwave," he recalls in the interview,

> that I could use this Chinese girl, whose house I would cycle by every day on our way from our cottage into town. I asked her if she would let me make drawings of her on [her] horse.

> We started doing this [but] the horse moved around a lot, so I simply then — knowing what I wanted the eye level to be and everything — I simply had her repeatedly ride around while I took photographs

with a polaroid camera. The results "were put into a geometric schema" with his ideas about the cross. Even his process of authenticating the horse and rider with photographs is less important than the mathematical perfection of the final image.

French Cross presents a powerful and multilayered evocation of memory. It is, of course, a record of Colville's visual thinking, especially of his idea to put the woman and the cross together. It is also a revisitation of the cross as a marker of the forced migration of the Acadian people and the loss of much French culture in Nova Scotia. But what of the woman's thoughts? In conversation, Colville stresses her racial derivation (half Chinese, half Caucasian), but in the picture we can't easily know that she also represents migration, in this case of her father, a Chinese professor of mathematics at Acadia University. Yet her gaze at the cross, even though she is well past it as her horse walks on, underlines the theme of looking back, of recollection. Colville has us meditate on origins and displacement as he shows her in accord with her environment. He affirms the importance of history and tradition by implying that our sense of belonging can be swiftly destroyed by events beyond our control, just as this sense of home was no doubt obliterated for the Acadian settlers, who in turn had displaced Aboriginal peoples. Ultimately *French Cross* depicts the changes that time inevitably and often tragically brings, and it emphasizes the need to remember its import by thinking historically.

CHOOSING TO BE POSITIVE

Colville affirms values that he holds dear, and though he is never tentative in person or in his art, neither is he dogmatic. His views stem not from a blind acceptance but from his experience, from aspects of life that he has authenticated, both through a painstaking process of technical verification and, equally important, through the filter of his philosophy. Clearly he harbours reservations about some of the themes that he depicts — potential violence, for example — but his work attempts to counteract negative values by presenting positive choices. Notwithstanding the subtlety and complexity of most of his art, we know where Colville stands when he presents a scene. Any ambiguity that we feel — for example, is the man considering violence in *Target Pistol and Man* (Fig. 4)? — is, for Colville, a necessary part of the theme, not a lack of resolution in his thinking or the image. As Burnett puts it, "ambiguities lie not in what we see but in how our seeing leads us to think" (27). Colville is thoroughly involved in what he does as both an artist and public figure. I am not simply reiterating the truism that he often uses himself as a model; Colville will only paint — or speak — about what he confidently understands, indeed, "that which one loves, respects, reveres, or is captivated by," as he puts it in Bruce's article. Thus, as viewers of his work or as interlocutors, we feel his presence, investment, and authority. We have something tangible about which to agree or disagree. It is in large measure this success in communication that makes Colville so popular.

His values are evident in his work and the choices that he has made as a person. We cannot miss his dedication to Rhoda: one of Colville's students from the early 1950s recalls that theirs was a real "romance," and this continues to be true. He employs Rhoda in many of his works; for him, if not for all contemporary viewers, it is a homage to her feminine mystery and their relationship. They spend as much time as possible together (see Fig. 18). Inscribed in his referencing of Rhoda is a specific view of relations between the sexes (as discussed in reference to *Western Star*), heterosexuality, and "family values." Colville's life and art also bespeak his rigorous personal routine. He is the sort of person by whom we can set our watches. His repetition of specific tasks — going to the post office, walking and grooming the family dog, painting every morning — is a way of reaffirming their importance. They are talismans against chaos. Moreover, Colville's serious undertaking of public duties affirms his belief in our responsibility toward society. There remains in him something of the would-be law student and politician. He values independence but is certainly not a recluse. Such pressing questions as whether cats in Wolfville should be leashed will find Colville the animal-lover speaking in a public forum. He has also found time to sit on the Museums Canada board, for example, or to be chancellor of Acadia University for over ten years. He has had rich experience in the facets of life that he most values. He lives and depicts these values, and whether we agree or disagree with them, we know who Alex Colville is and where he stands.

THE ART OF PHILOSOPHIZING

In 1986, Colville completed a serigraph called *Köln Express*. The title refers to the ship in the image, a vessel that Colville had seen from Point Pleasant Park in Halifax. This ship held his interest partly because of his associations with Köln (Cologne), Germany, where he has exhibited and where *Truck Stop* hangs in the prestigious Ludwig Museum. This work is also a favourite of Colville's because, as we have seen, he overcame the technical difficulties that it presented. The image is entirely ordinary in Colville's sense. Nothing dramatic is happening — recall his words about the war: "much of nothing" happens — though we notice a man lying on a park bench. Explicating this work for the audience at the University of Toronto Schools, however, Colville says something surprising. He mentions off-handedly that he sees the recumbent man as a "philosopher." We tend to imagine philosophers as grand people, perhaps with flowing beards or memorialized by a public sculpture or elaborate tomb. But Colville's philosopher is both alive and worldly. Although he is somewhat detached, he is a common man, someone with whom we can identify and communicate. This sort of philosopher —

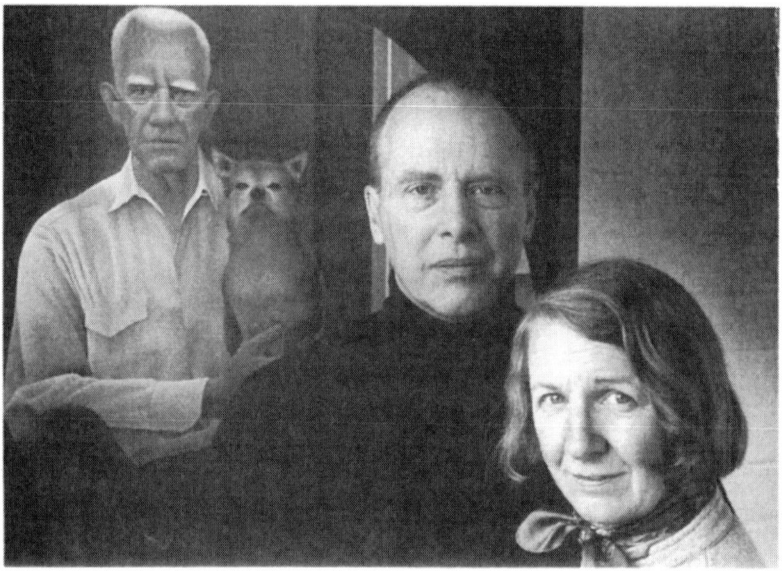

FIGURE 18

Portrait of Alex and Rhoda Colville by Guido Mangold, Germany, 1977: behind them hangs Colville's My Father with His Dog *(1968).*

and philosophy — is important to Colville, and he often incorporates them in his images. He likens *Köln Express* to an earlier work, *Ocean Limited* (1962), because in both we see "a large functioning machine [a ship and train, respectively] and a (practically) non-functioning person," as Colville writes in a letter dated 9 December 1992. More exactly, the machines are active, whereas the philosopher is contemplative, an aloof observer who doesn't directly participate in the action, but who thinks about its implications (a type that Burnett rightly identifies in many of Colville's images [148, 152]). Significantly, as Colville notes in the letter, the philosopher in the more recent picture is modelled on his physical appearance.

Colville is this sort of philosophical artist, one who ponders the big questions of life and tries to address them in his work without pretension or specialized language. "There *are* these basic questions," he insists in Burnett's monograph:

> "What's it all about?"; "What's happening?"; "What is life like?" Of course there are no specific answers to these questions, perhaps no answers at all, but people who work with this sort of question in mind do tend, I suggest, to produce work which is interesting to some people who do not have a special interest in the visual arts. (18)

Colville's concern with, and success in, the communication of his ideas about such questions are fundamental factors in his popularity, and his ideas do make him a contemporary German Romantic. "People in the arts have something in common with philosophers," he asserts in his address. "I don't mean to say that artists *are* [necessarily] philosophers," but both look for "the meaning of life, the essential," because they believe that life isn't meaningless or banal. Colville's is an art of philosophizing, of thinking through and presenting ideas in a popular, communicative manner. Like the man on the bench — though it's hard to imagine him being so informal — he is a philosopher among us, in this world.

We have examined important aspects of Colville's philosophy, but I want to look here at several more principles — philosophies, in the popular sense — that are basic to his character and animate his art. In general, these principles are moral and ethical, directed toward our way of existing with others in society. Although Colville's intellectual interests are broad — ranging to science, poetry, and psychology — most crucial to an understanding of the man are his views on religion, nature (animals particularly), and what we call the Humanities, fields of inquiry closely related to his life's work: art history, literature, and philosophy. An investigation of these areas amounts to an intellectual biography of Colville. Because he is profoundly serious and intellectual, an understanding of these influences in his life brings us closest to him.

RELIGION AND SPIRITUALITY

Undoubtedly Colville is interested in Christianity and religion in general. He speaks about "grace," for example, and his approach to ethical issues could be called religious. But he is less and less concerned with organized religion; concomitantly his work deals with spiritual themes rather than specifically religious ones. *Chaplain* (1991) is more about a friend than about his office. The rightly famous *Dog and Priest* (1978) — in which Colville, dressed in black like a priest, has his eyes and identifying collar obscured by those of his dog — can easily be seen to question how much religious people *see* in the philosophical sense. Helen Dow's monograph on Colville pushes religious readings of his work up to the early '70s as far as one can. Colville still thinks that she was on to something about him and his art: "There is in me some kind of religious residue," he says in the interview. "I think Helen Dow really zeroed in on this." He regrets the poor press that this aspect of her book received. At the same time, he doesn't reject Burnett's rebuttals of Dow's interpretations (167–71).

One way to appreciate Colville's present feelings about religion is through a humorous story he tells. On 9 November 1992, he received in the mail a large cardboard tube from Ottawa. He wasn't expecting it and couldn't guess its contents. Intrigued, he opened it and discovered his official certificate as a new member of the Privy Council. Then came the story, told in Rhoda's presence. Informed that he was to be honoured with membership in this elite body, Colville was later briefed on the ceremony, conducted in the presence of Queen Elizabeth on 1 July 1992. As he relates in the interview,

> Someone from Rideau Hall [the governor general's residence] phoned and said [that] "Part of this ceremony that you'll be involved in tomorrow involves receiving a Bible, which will be signed by the queen. For this reason, we want to know what your religion is." I said, well, actually I don't have a religion. [Rhoda interjects: "I think that was a foolish thing (to say)!"] The woman said, "That's no problem." [The next day,] when we all assembled in Rideau Hall, the [organizer said,] "You'll find on a table there a Bible with your name on it, and when you go into the big room for the ceremony, take it with you." I went to look and said I couldn't find one. They said, "You'll get a piece of paper signed by the queen," which is what happened.

No religion, no Bible from the queen! Colville seems content, though, to have paid the price for independence of mind. He remains interested in, and respectful of, religious ideas but is nonetheless "inclined to think that no man who is a real artist can be religious in this day and age," as he says in Johnson's article.

"AN EX-SEMI-CATHOLIC"

Colville is "lapsed." He was "processed as a Catholic," as he colourfully puts it in Johnson's article, but is now "an ex-semi-Catholic" from a family in which his mother was Catholic and his father Protestant, as he notes in the interview. At a young age, he was aware of both the class-oriented nature and spiritual dimensions of organized faiths. "My mother was ambitious for my brother and me," he reports. Because she knew "instinctively" that being a Catholic in Nova Scotia "would not be a plus in terms of socio-economic" opportunity, she always "found excuses for not sending us to Catholic schools."

Although he and Robert had begun school in Ontario, his early secular education in the Maritimes was the reason for a temporary conversion to Catholicism. Because he hadn't had religious training in school, when it came time for his first communion, he had to be instructed by a team of travelling priests. He remembers going to special classes after school for this purpose at twelve or thirteen. He was captivated: "I was actually at a certain point a very devout kid. . . . I was very serious about [religion] as an adolescent. It faded out later, and by the time I was in university, it was *gone*!" Perhaps devoutness diminished as he matured, but students remember Colville attending church with his family at Mount Allison (affiliated with the United Church of Canada). Colville maintains that he attended mainly for the sake of Rhoda and their children: "the kids went to United Church Sunday school. Even I went [to church] occasionally." But he didn't really belong. A student from Mount Allison recalls that Colville was "disdainful" in the early '50s about the theology being taught there and about religion generally. "Disdainful would be quite accurate," Colville laughs today. "With one exception, the ministers that were [in Sackville] I thought were poor." But he doesn't leave the topic on this negative note. There are "good people in the Divinity College here at Acadia," he says, musing that perhaps the education for ministers and the people drawn to this vocation have improved. There remains, then, a "religious residue" in Colville, a sensitivity to ethical questions and a sense of public mission.

Colville also finds spiritual value in nature, specifically in animals, usually domestic ones that he has known or at least observed closely. Animals have always been part of his life, and they appear in more than a third of his works. Their presence is by no means entirely religious, but there is a connection. Burnett quotes Colville as saying, in 1982,

> I saw an article by a woman in a religious commune in which she said they had three rules, no liquor, no drugs, and no dogs. I thought this was very strange, because to me the presence of animals seems absolutely necessary. I feel that without animals everything is incomplete (157).

But why are animals special and necessary, even in a religious community? Colville further claims, "I think of animals as being incapable of evil, and I certainly don't think this about people" (157), as we've seen in his statement about how Germans discovered the potential for evil during the Nazi period. The answer lies in the differences between animals and people. For Colville, animals are innocent. They are ignorant of our motives, yet they are often closely involved with us, whether as pets or livestock. They are good; we may or may not be. Colville also sees animals as independent, a quality that he highly values. Although pets may interact with us constantly, we do not know much about their emotions or instincts. In a sense, they are superior to us because they follow nature's laws and harmonies. At the same time, we seek (at our best) to protect animals, to care for them, as Burnett points out (167). The relationship is one of power, of the strong protecting the innocent, a crucial theme in Colville's works. The Colvilles come by their pets in this way, too: the dog that we see on the cover was rescued from being put down by its former owner; their Siamese cat came from a neighbour who could no longer care for it. This close identification with animals — dogs especially — is conscious. Asked by Dow about the pet in *Woman and Terrier* (1963), Colville claims, "I thought of it as a kind of Madonna and Child, or 'Holy Terrier' as I sometimes called it." Later, Dow reports, he even felt that "essentially I *am* the dog," held close in the woman's arms, yet clearly animated by independent thoughts. Some people who know Colville think of him as somehow canine. Shih likened his method of making art to a dog chewing a bone, and Godard has described him as a Labrador (a breed that Colville has owned). To explain her intuition, she points out how "very much part of the household" dogs and cats are to the Colvilles, and we think of *Refrigerator*. The animals and house are "secure, comfortable, peaceful [with] no surprises," which is how Godard sees Colville, as she admits in an interview on 15 December 1992.

ANIMALS

Colville depicts animals both alone and with humans. In *Moon and Cow* (Fig. 12), he portrays the perfect interchange between the cow and its setting; one literally reflects the other's patterns, and there is symmetry and peace, perhaps even what Colville calls "grace." We assume that the cow knows nothing about the shelter built for it and shown in the distance. Yet it represents the care of domesticated animals. Their harmony with the world is, for Colville, an anchor amidst the chaos of human affairs, a cause for hope.

This hope is both literal and symbolic. Colville shows animals truly at rest and contented. He depicts their essence, the truth of their existence. His avowed concern with the "ontological," as he writes in "Statement" — with the realm of being and beings in the world — also finds important expression in his images of animals as symbolic of a larger harmony. "But I have a strong conviction that *things are there* whether we respond to them or not," he writes, and he is careful to show the potential for goodness in the animal world. This symbolic function guided his choice of animals for Canada's centennial coins. About the one-cent piece, he writes in "Alex Colville on His Centennial Coins": "For this I wished to use a very common bird, but one with symbolic overtones. I selected the dove (rock dove) — very common, in cities as well as the country . . . and having associations with spiritual values and also with peace." While Colville is serious about this symbolism, there is a lighter (and biting) side

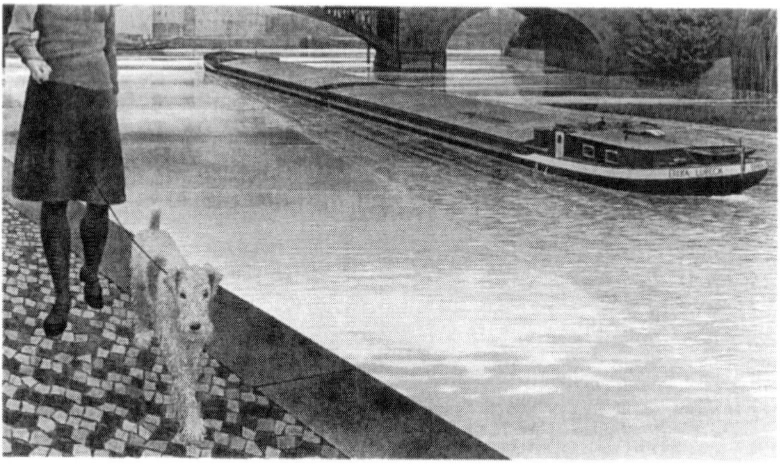

FIGURE 19

Colville, The River Spree *(1971): acrylic polymer emulsion, 60 x 104 cm., collection of Ludwig Forum für internationale kunst, Aachen, Germany.*

to his choice of animals. "When I designed and made the models for the . . . centennial coins," he reports in "A Tribute," "I could not find any person admirable enough to be commemorated (no Jefferson, Grant, or Roosevelt) so I used (commemorated) six animals."

His symbolism can also be more lugubrious, as in the famous *Seven Crows* (1980), which, as Burnett points out, is based partly on the traditional rhyme:

One crow sorrow,
Two crows joy,
Three crows a letter,
Four crows a boy,
Five crows silver,
Six crows gold,
Seven crows a story never to be told. (174)

It is also based on the nineteenth-century Swiss painter Arnold Böcklin's (1827–1901) forbidding *Island of the Dead* (1880). In *Seven Crows*, Colville uses animals to explore one of his philosophical preoccupations, the constant proximity of death. It is thus likely that somewhere in his mind when he imagined this image was van Gogh's famous late painting *Crows over the Wheat Field* (1890), in which the birds are frequently seen as harbingers of van Gogh's imminent death.

Colville is often pictured with various pets, both in biographical photos — such as that taken of him in 1991 walking near Wolfville with the family dog (cover) — and in his art. *Dog and Priest* (1978) provides an excellent example not only of his habit of "obscuring" portraits but also of the relationship between people and animals, one of both intimacy and alterity. The dog *sees* for the man: human eyes are replaced by canine eyes. But we don't know what the dog sees in any but the most literal sense. In this image, the animal stands in for a human function — seeing in the sense of understanding — but also implies the limit, and perhaps futility, of spiritual insight. The dramatic family portrait taken in 1977 by Guido Mangold — a German photographer whom the Colvilles were visiting and who owns the painting that we see in the background (Fig. 18) — poses similar questions about seeing. Alex and Rhoda stand in front of the painting *My Father with His Dog* (1968). All four "Colvilles" look out calmly yet somewhat intensely. Perhaps more than the other figures, the dog exudes with its body language the sense of upright independence evinced by the group. This sense goes beyond the cliché of people looking like their pets, though the dog and elder Colville do share prominent ears, eyes, and downturned mouths. Again, the animal works as an image of a larger whole, in this case the family portrait. The animal is part of the genealogy, but the mystery of its otherness remains because it is held within the family circle.

Although not in the same breath, Colville has claimed that both animals and women are ultimately unknowable. This quality raises them in his estimation, and many of his images showing animals with people focus on the relationship between a woman — usually modelled on Rhoda — and a pet. A partial list includes *Woman and Terrier* (1963), *The River Spree* (1971; Fig. 19), *Cyclist and Crow* (1981), *Woman, Dog, and Canoe* (1982), and *Stove* (1988). Colville doesn't imply that women have a particular ability to communicate with animals. He emphasizes that a dog, for example, has its own existence, even when it's walking while leashed, as in *The River Spree* (Fig. 19). This deceptively tranquil work resulted from the Colvilles' stay in Berlin in 1971. We see the river Spree — which cuts through what were then East and West Berlin and thus became a politicized passageway through the Berlin Wall and even the Iron Curtain — and a barge, travelling away from us. Rhoda walks Shasta, the terrier, who knows nothing of the political symbolism of the spot. By contrast, Colville, who, we know, dislikes apolitical people, trusts that we will catch the drift of the painting, the sense that apparent calm and quotidian activity may mask a volatile political situation. As Colville suggests, animals may not be acquainted with evil. Their fortunate ignorance throws our potential for violence and cruelty into relief.

Colville derives much pleasure and inspiration from his knowledge of art history, literature, and philosophy. It's time to look at his interest in these areas. His affinities with other artists, authors, and thinkers frequently illuminate (and are sometimes sources for) some of his salient traits and beliefs. Colville maintains a paradoxical relationship with art history: on the one hand, he is knowledgeable about, and fascinated by, art of the past. Yet he remains aloof from most contemporary practice and keeps his distance from other artists and the art world. Does he therefore live in the past? Not really, for he claims to be a vital part of the Western artistic tradition. In another of his disarmingly yet revealing remarks, for example, Colville says that he sees himself "as belonging to [art] history" — and this sentiment existed before he became an international celebrity. In 1984 he recalled, in "The World," that "I once said to a dealer I had in New York twenty years ago, 'I am the locomotive of art history,' punning on the remark that [Soviet leader] Khrushchev made in one of his crazy speeches. . . . I know this sounds pretentious, but I don't believe in false modesty." The "locomotive" reference implies his recognition that his realist style was, especially in the '50s and '60s, out of favour, eclipsed and made anachronistic by contemporary abstract expressionism in the United States and abstract painting in Canada. "Even as a very young painter," Colville recalls in Bruce's article, "I knew I was living in a world that was hostile to my work. . . . You were going against the grain. . . . Unless you were adroit, society would flatten you out." Yet he was sure of his chosen direction, and, indeed, his tenacious fidelity to a realist practice *has* ensured him a place in art history.

Colville has the reputation of being uninterested in other art, but it is more accurate to say that he is just selective in his attention. His tastes are more catholic than the stereotyped view of him allows. He has always gone out of his way to see historical art. At the end of World War II, for example, he went to see a collection of van Gogh's early work in the possession of the

Dutchman's nephew. Around this time, he also visited the Louvre in Paris, and while he was struck by the work of Edouard Manet (1832–83), "The thing that hit me hardest was the ancient Egyptian art [in which] . . . the main theme . . . is death, eternity, and all that business," as he puts it in Bruce's article. In retrospect, at least, he thinks that he's had a longstanding passion for this type of art. His first contacts with art were at the Royal Ontario Museum in Toronto, where, as a teenager, he saw ancient Egyptian art with his maternal grandfather, "a tailor with a meditative mind," as he writes in Burnett's monograph (15). Colville's interest in this unusual trio of artistic directions — van Gogh, Manet, and ancient Egyptian relief sculpture — encapsulates his philosophy about relating to past art. "All real artist[s] are brothers and co-workers in different generations . . . ," he wrote in "Statement." Burnett, in the interview, confirms that Colville still holds this view. In fact, the idea that "the whole of art history should be used" by the contemporary artist — instead of focusing on other current productions — is Colville's "different way of looking at one's professionalism" as an artist.

PATTERNS OF INTEREST

In a 1978 interview with Gilles Toupin, published in Montreal's *La Presse*, Colville claimed that he "knows and thinks a lot about the history of art," but that he works "as if modern art didn't exist" (my translation). He has been markedly influenced by early art, but he continues to go his own way. Over the years — in interviews, statements, and lectures — he has recorded many of his art-historical affinities. If we compile a partial list of these references, we can glean patterns of interest and recognize consistent sore points. Colville hasn't ignored modern art as much as he suggests. He likes Italian painting of the early Renaissance period, particularly the work of artists such as Piero della Francesca (c. 1410–92), whose clarity of vision and pictorial construction Colville reflects in our time. He admires other artists from various epochs who share these qualities: the French classicist Nicolas Poussin (1594–1665), Jan Vermeer, the Dutch painter of domestic interior scenes (1632–75), and Georges Seurat (1859–91), the French painter who perfected the technique of "divisionism," whereby a strong effect of colour is obtained not by mixing pigments on the canvas but by placing complimentary colours close to one another so that the optical mixing takes place in the viewers' eyes. Colville learned this technique from Stanley Royle at Mount Allison and continues to employ a version of it. Surprisingly, perhaps, Colville also lists several sculptors in his pantheon of great artists: the American pop artist George Segal (1924–), the English Henry Moore (1898–1986), and Donatello (c. 1386–1466) from the Italian Renaissance. Colville shares with them a concern for placing the figure in a convincing three-dimensional space, even though he must employ a one-point perspective (itself a Renaissance invention) to accomplish this illusion on a flat surface. Also crucial to Colville is the American realist tradition, exemplified by Thomas Eakins (1844–1916), and continued, though in different veins, by Edward Hopper (1882–1967), George Tooker (1920–), and Ben Shahn (1898–1969). Shahn's work in particular prompted Colville to visit New York galleries in the early 1950s. Some of these artists' works had been shown in 1950 at the Hewitt Gallery in New York, under the title "Symbolic Realism," the same venue in which Colville had his first important exhibition in 1952, Burnett points out (112). Colville sees these and other American artists as his immediate predecessors and feels, therefore, that the tag of regional artist, often applied to him because of his rootedness in the Maritimes, is misleading.

Several of these influences are modern, though not avant-garde or strictly modernist, terms that suggest new directions such as abstraction and surrealism. Colville admires the dream-like, surrealist work of the Belgian painter Paul Delvaux (1897–), which we see in *Nude and Dummy* (1950; Fig. 14). I have also noted Colville's attachment to Max Beckmann's expressionistic self-portraits, but on the whole, he cares little for the more radical strains of twentieth-century art. The same holds for recent Canadian art. He admires the robust canvases of Goodrich Roberts (1904–74), the wartime work of Will Ogilvie (1901–), and the cool, precise, yet mysterious canvases of Winnipeg painter LeMoine Fitzgerald (1890–1956). As we might expect, he's also impressed by the rigorous conceptual and technical qualities of paintings by both Mary and Christopher Pratt (both b. 1935); indeed, he taught Mary Pratt at Mount Allison, and she continues to find him an inspiration. He has written an approving preface to a catalogue of work by the Ontario artist Jeremy Smith (1946–). Among contemporary Canadians in the visual arts, then, there are no k.d. langs for Colville, and no surprises for those who know his tastes.

DISLIKES IN ART

Colville is more likely to speak about what he is excited by than about what he dislikes, but he has occasionally mentioned artists and periods of art that he doesn't endorse or appreciate. Of the movements, abstract art and the emotional work of the seventeenth-century Counter-Reformation in Europe stand out. As we have seen, when he was a member of the National Gallery of Canada's acquisitions committee, he voted against the planned purchase of Barnett Newman's monumental *Voice of Fire* (1967). About the work of Jack Bush (1909–77) — one of Canada's leading abstractionists — he admits in "The World" that he just can't see the point: "Someplace I used to go to meetings there was a big Bush — and a good one — on the wall and I would look at it for hours listening to people talk and it just didn't register on me." But he's humble rather than censorious: "everybody doesn't like everything. . . . It's just the limitation that any individual has." He is consistent in his likes and dislikes but not necessarily predictable. We can understand his dismissal of the Group of Seven, whose philosophy of art diverged from Colville's, yet he doesn't necessarily appreciate the work of all other realists. "For instance," he says in "The World," "I don't like [Ken] Danby's [1940–] work. I'm not knocking Danby. . . . [But] I find it a bit annoying that some people think that because I'm a realist I automatically like the things that other realist painters do. I don't." Typically Colville is discerning in his choices of ancestors and mentors from art history, which provides him with material for his success, the templates, we might say, for his image as a self-made man. He claims in "Statement" to have learned from the French thinker André Malraux that "the initial impulse to be an artist comes not from the contemplation of nature but from the contemplation of other art." Colville continues to define himself through his affinities with others' art and in creating his own.

Corroborating this observation is the formal interest in art history that Colville developed as a teacher at Mount Allison. He first used Helen Gardner's influential survey *Art through the Ages*. He claims in Burnett's monograph to have been affected by the American art historian Bernard Berenson's writings (55), likely because Berenson also favours the painting of the Italian Renaissance and praises the connoisseur's practice of looking closely at art. Later, Colville employed Ernst Gombrich's *The Story of Art*, a famous text that champions the rise of realist painting. But Colville is not always the conservative that we expect him to be. In the interview, he claims to have been fascinated by a radical book by art historian Michael Fried. *Realism, Writing, Disfiguration: On Thomas Eakins and Stephen Crane* (1987) brings together Colville's interest in American realist art (Eakins) and the novel (Crane). Colville is happy to learn from a range of sources in art and art history alike. His selective affinities only strengthen his aesthetic ideals and make him more the person he seeks to be.

THE READER OF NOVELS

Colville is an avid reader of fiction and nonfiction, but of all his intellectual pursuits, his passion for the novel is paramount. When asked why he derives both satisfaction and stimulation from philosophical and literary sources, he responds, in a letter dated 30 January 1993, by demonstrating yet again his mastery of the seemingly tangential anecdote. "Some writer (I forget who)," quips Colville, "has said that he reads science, and went on to say, 'A cow eats grass and produces milk' — so the production of [visual] art requires the consumption of something else." Colville regularly makes time in his daily routine for such stimulation. As a result, he is well-read, and his work is literary in important ways.

Before considering possible influences from, and affinities with, some of the many authors in whom Colville is interested, I stress that we should not insult his intellect by simply looking for literary sources for his images. What Colville finds in his favourite authors is a confirmation or elaboration of his beliefs about life, morality, and art. So while we can and should ask questions about his relationship to the narrative techniques of Joseph Conrad (1857–1924), for example, we must remember that Colville is a man of ideas, which he uses in his unique, visual context. In 1951, he announced this emphasis in "My Experience": "I . . . placed all my bets, so to speak, on a . . . rigorous, disciplined, and intellectual plan of attack, a plan which relied less on perception, though perception was involved in it, and more on *conception*" (emphasis added). As he says in Toupin's article, literature has helped him to discover a "language" in which to conceptualize life's most serious questions. An abridged list of Colville's favourite literary authors and works, then, is only a prelude to a discussion of the questions that he asks in their company.

One of his earliest passions was the writing of T.E. Lawrence (1888–1935) — better known as Lawrence of Arabia — whose gallant adventure tales he enjoyed in his teens. Also of his parents' generation was the British writer Ford Madox Ford (1873–1939), whose massive novel *Parade's End* (1950) he discovered in 1968. Dow quotes him as saying,

> I was deeply, enormously impressed with it. Very few people have read it, and one rarely sees references to it. This indi-

cates that works of the highest order can exist as "sleepers" — known only to a few people. I think Ford must have known that he had done something really good when he finished this . . . in his mid-fifties. He died an obscure academic in Michigan in 1939. There is perhaps a lesson in this.

The "lesson"? There are several, at least as we look back at Colville's reactions to Ford's work. Colville achieved what he considered success at fifty, in 1970, and achievement in his field had preoccupied him. "[W]hen I went to art school," he wrote in "My Experience," "my chief concern was whether I was good enough to be a success; I wondered if there would be any student who would be 'better' than I was." Colville is aware that his realist proclivities set him against the mainstream of "progressive" contemporary art. In this context, his elevated place in art history — established now for about two decades — makes him a "sleeper," too. As Burnett points out, Ford's combination of British and American perspectives might also have endeared him to Colville, keenly aware of both his Scottish heritage and position as quintessentially North American and Canadian (139). In addition, Ford's novel focuses on the collapse of moral values around the time of World War II, a theme close to Colville's interests. Like other authors whom Colville admires, Ford also wrote criticism, specifically on narrative technique. And he collaborated with, and wrote a biography of, one of Colville's main inspirations, Joseph Conrad.

Colville often mentions Conrad, and it's not difficult to understand their affinity, for the author of such famous works as *Lord Jim* and *Heart of Darkness* combined detailed, realistic description with a romantic concern for characters in moral dilemmas. Colville is also interested in the ways that Conrad's narratives invite us to identify with his characters and enter the stories. Two other British authors have particularly inspired Colville: the poet, dramatist, and critic T.S. Eliot (1888–1965), and the novelist and philosopher Iris Murdoch (1919–), whom Colville met and with whom he keeps in touch. Eliot's influence on Colville has been significant. In his 1951 artist's statement "My Experience," he paraphrased Eliot's notion that "all *great* literature deals with universal problems and concepts (in other words, it has extrinsic value), but that whether or not a piece of writing is literature at all must be determined on the basis of its intrinsic qualities as a work of art." Colville's art could well be described in these terms, for it maintains a balance between intrinsic order and extrinsic implication. Murdoch's many novels — Colville has read them all — are notable for portraying characters in situations that control them, in showing their lack of freedom of choice. Accidental occurrences, chance encounters — these phenomena are also important in Colville's work (for instance, in *Traveller* [1992; Fig. 8], in which the driver's chance confrontation with a hitchhiker can lead to all sorts of moral and metaphysical speculation), though he is more inclined to emphasize our ability to choose or fashion our lives. Colville has actually been more affected by Murdoch's philosophical writings.

After the war, Colville read James Joyce (1882–1941), the expatriate Irish writer. Dow quotes him as saying about Joyce:

> "Ulysses" I have always thought a modern masterpiece, and "Portrait of the Artist as a Young Man" is also really good. Hemingway, whose work I always admired, admired Joyce, and thoroughly respected him. I think "Finnegans Wake," though wonderfully witty and of great formal intricacy, is really a failure — too private and obscure. I think Joyce made a mistake, perhaps an inevitable one, in becoming an expatriate — there is a play by him [*Exiles*] (not well known) in which this problem is central, but I think his leaving the environment he knew so well eventually resulted in his work becoming what I would call over-abstract, lacking in the concrete and specific. My interest in Joyce . . . was probably due to my sharing with him a provincial background, also the ex-Catholic business. . . .

The hermetic qualities of *Finnegans Wake* are indeed antithetical to Colville's desire to communicate with his "readers." In Burnett's study, he describes his artistic method as "the working out, or the clarification and concretizing of some sort of trauma, which is my trauma," one that works, potentially, "for the person who looks at the painting" (92). Equally central to his philosophy of life is his rootedness in the Maritimes, his desire to know what's going on. While Colville shares with Joyce an ambivalence — to say the least — about Catholicism, his ascription of Joyce's "over-abstraction" to his dislocation from Ireland is perhaps a case of projection, of Colville's affirmation of *his* sense of self. Joyce felt that he had to leave his homeland; Colville, in contrast, needed the familiarity of boyhood, especially after his disorientation and loneliness overseas during World War II. "Because of my perplexity" after the war, he wrote in "My Experience,"

> and because, rather to my surprise, I discovered that I was very strongly attached to the Maritimes, I decided to settle down in Sackville where I could have the time, the feeling of belonging, the solitude and, above all, the freedom from distraction which I needed to become oriented as an artist.

Colville's attachment to the work of Ernest Hemingway (1899–1961) is not difficult to understand given the American writer's terse, descriptive style and interest in human character. He also reads works by Saul Bellow (1915–) and John Updike (1932–). Colville's interest not only in the novels of a writer such as Updike but also in his less-known critical essays on art and literature is unusual. Also significant to Colville is the trilogy of the American writer John dos Passos (1896–1970), which travels through the early decades of twentieth-century United States. Published in the 1930s, *The 42nd Parallel, Nineteen Nineteen*, and *The Big Money* construct a sweeping picture of American life from a conservative vantage point that would appeal to Colville. The American perspective on life is also crucial to him because he feels a part more of North American than of Maritime culture, despite his affinity for the place that he knows best. In

"A Tribute," he describes his "sense of being distinctly North American. . . . Both as a painter and as a person I see myself as one whose life and work involve issues, and take place in contexts, which no European (and more obviously no Asian) has experienced." In keeping with this view, he is typically outspoken, in "The World," about the label of regionalism that is often applied to his work: "I object to [the idea] and think it is foolish. One of the things that I like about Burnett's analysis of my work is that it pretty well destroys this idea."

Other writers in English important to Colville are the Russian-born Vladimir Nabokov (1899–1977) and the Canadian novelist Alice Munro (1931–), whose seemingly simple and direct stories of life in rural Ontario mask a complexity and strangeness also found in Colville's mysterious images. Also influential were the French existentialists Jean-Paul Sartre (1905–80) and Albert Camus (1913–60), whose works Colville read in translation in the 1940s and '50s, and who were "enormously significant in a way I don't think anyone could comprehend today," Burnett quotes him as saying (55). Furthermore, he has appreciated the novels of the French man of letters André Malraux — whose writings on art were also instrumental to his sense of art history — and the work of Thomas Mann (1875–1955) and Leo Tolstoy (1828–1910).

LITERATURE AND MORALITY

Is it possible to find a common thread in Colville's literary interests? Despite the range of his reading, he is consistent in his attraction to works that focus on human character, on dilemmas — "traumas," to use his term — and development in the face of adversity. Colville is interested in *moral* literature not as a source for his images but as confirmation of a moral worldview that he seeks to articulate visually. He suggests in Toupin's article that he is an optimist in everyday life, but that his view of the human condition is less sanguine. His art thus runs parallel to the literature that he reads, portraying some of the same issues, the same human condition. Both his literary interests and his art come from this "something else."

If literature doesn't truly provide the sources of Colville's work, then in what sense are his paintings and serigraphs literary? There are strong *narrative* qualities in his work — qualities of authorial control and opinion — that make many viewers want to "read" a Colville image as part of a story. Burnett has tried to counter this view, suggesting that Colville's sense of time, and the differences between his work and photography, obviate the possibility that his works are like literature in their narrativity. Discussing *Horse and Train* (1954), Burnett writes that Colville "had to avoid a sense of narrative, and he removed the image from the natural flow of time to prevent common sense from projecting the confrontation of horse and train to a disastrous conclusion" (100). It is true, as Burnett also claims, that "The momentary state that a photograph records is selected out of time; we can reconstruct the moments before and the moments after," but it does not follow for all or even many of Colville's works that "we cannot construct . . . a narrative that will satisfy the actual fact of the painting" (226). As I have frequently witnessed in the remarks of people looking at Colville's images, such a "narrative" reconstruction is exactly what most viewers are after and is what intrigues and satisfies them about his work. The ability to supply a narrative is also what makes Colville's art so literary.

Burnett is scrupulous about the famous *Horse and Train* because it is one of the few works in Colville's oeuvre that is based directly on a literary model, a poem called "Dedication to Mary Campbell," published by South African writer Roy Campbell in 1949. Burnett quotes the lines in question: "Against a regiment I oppose a brain / And a dark horse against an armoured train" (97). Interestingly, too, Campbell's autobiography is entitled *Light on a Dark Horse* (1951). Colville recognizes the differences between the written and visual arts. But because time is expressed differently in paintings than in novels — spatially and (more or less) at once, rather than sequentially — does not mean that we as viewers or Colville as an artist must "avoid a sense of narrative," as Burnett argues (100). Photographs are usually (though not necessarily) composed differently than Colville's long-gestated images, but again this does not imply that photography is a narrative art whereas Colville's work is not.

That a viewer supplies a narrative depends little on Colville's methods for conceiving and constructing a picture. Most people who see *French Cross* (Fig. 3), for example, aren't aware that the cross and young woman weren't originally — and aren't in fact — placed together. They are contiguous in the image, and viewers try to explain this fact. The recourse to a narrative — whether or not it's a story imagined by Colville — is a crucial part of that "communication" with his audience so fundamental to him. George Grant (1918–88), a philosopher and friend of the Colvilles, once wrote to Colville about *Truck Stop* (1966), and Colville suggests in "A Tribute" that his words were "perhaps the most complimentary . . . ever made to me about my work":

> The painting shows the central part of a Mack cab-over-engine eighteen wheel truck at an Esso station in the early morning. . . . The pump attendant has a broken arm in a cast in a sling. A German shepherd dog is smelling one of the tires of the truck. George wrote me that this painting was something he and his fourteen-year-old son could contemplate in silent rapport.

Isn't this "silent rapport" the pleasure of narrative, of finding, and identifying with, a story?

To suggest that Colville's images are imbued with narrative elements by viewers is not to claim that he narrates the scenes that he constructs. By the same token, though he is careful to depict only what he understands, not all that he shows is his experience. He creates fictions, just as the novelists that he admires do. Paul Eakin, a theorist of autobiography, argues persuasively that "the self that is the center of all autobiographical narrative is necessarily a fictive structure." He goes on to claim that storytelling — which Colville readily undertakes in his work and conversation — is actually a "drive toward narration of the self," toward what I have been calling self-fashioning. As beholders of Colville's work, we also create fictions of content and narrative; we make up a story, a fact that Colville willingly embraces. "We can never discount the experience of the viewer," he claims in "The World." While remembering that his images — even those that include his features — are not in any simple, empirical sense just him, we need to recall the degree to which he, more than most artists, constructs and controls the pictures that we see. While he doesn't give us a narrative "solution," as Burnett fears those interested in his stories might (26), he does construct a definite point of view, a physical and moral *perspective*.

He provides this perspective partly through the visual means for which he has become justly famous: rigorous mathematical measurement and balancing, the exclusion of extraneous detail, and an overall simplicity and identifiability in the characters and situations shown. In addition, however, Colville's ability to structure a scene so that we see it through his eyes results from his combination of visual and more literary techniques. His simple titles, for example, form narratives from which it's difficult to waver. Many of his titles, such as *Target Pistol and Man* (Fig. 4), are binary —the terms are held together for comparison. It's not that Colville sees the world as simple, either physically or metaphysically; he's not a reductive thinker but one who aims at concentrated statements, at essentials. Many of his titles are also comprised of a single word that tells us little and leaves the image mysterious but that nonetheless decides a point of view in advance. A recent example is *Traveller* (Fig. 8).

In this haunting work, we see through the eyes of the traveller in the car, modelled on Colville in his Porsche 911. We catch a glimpse of the other traveller, a hitchhiker who gestures from the verge, but we don't stop to pick him (or her?) up. The speedometer registers sixty kilometres per hour as we drive past. The title directs our attention to the connections and disjunctions between these travellers, one in the car, one on the road. Without presenting an answer, Colville depicts this scene so that certain existential questions and dilemmas arise in our minds. Who is the hitchhiker? Do we have a moral responsibility toward him or her?

Colville has said that he's not interested in personality — his own or others' — and his depiction here is not designed to make us think about Alex Colville specifically. Using his features and experience, he universalizes (or at least generalizes) and lets us into the image. His method of distilling images and ideas over time finds corroboration in the theories of T.S. Eliot. For Eliot, in an essay entitled "Tradition and the Individual Talent," an artist (he speaks of poets, but the point can be extended) should be interested not in personality or immediate emotional experiences but in "a particular medium, which is only a medium and not a personality, [and] in which impressions and experiences combine in peculiar and unexpected ways." To understand the medium, the artist needs what Eliot calls a "historical sense" of its past, in Colville's case, the history of art. "This historical sense," Eliot claims, "which is the sense of the timeless as well as of the temporal and of the timeless and the temporal together, is what makes a writer traditional." Colville's work can well be described as evoking the timeless and temporal together. He accomplishes this end by visual and literary means, some found in Eliot's essays, including this one, which Colville read in the 1950s, as he notes in a letter dated 30 January 1993. Colville also remembers Eliot's distinction between "the mind which creates and the man who suffers," the difference between merely individual and potentially inaccessible personality and the transcendent values of the medium.

THE WORLDLY PHILOSOPHER

I began this section with an analysis of *Köln Express*, the serigraph in which Colville pictures himself as a worldly philosopher pondering reality while acting within it. Of all the inspirations for his art, this conception of philosophy and the philosopher has been the most influential, indicative of whom Colville aspires to be and has, for the most part, become. Commemorating the life and work of Canadian philosopher and political scientist George Grant in 1989, Colville writes in "A Tribute": "philosophy has a kind of fascination for me. . . . I think there are more connections than current society acknowledges between academe, the realm of abstract thought, and the arts, which are, in a sense, the realm of action, at least the realm of ideated action. . . ." A felicitous term that Colville derives from Berenson's phrase "ideated sensation," "ideated action" is a notion that combines ideation and action, both the action of constructing works of art and, more significantly, the *moral* agency of these works in the world. For Colville, "the aim of art is to illuminate and enhance the human condition," as he says in a 1962 statement contained in the Helen J. Dow Fonds.

Colville has always demonstrated a philosophical cast of mind. We recall his interest as a teenager in theology, for example, or witness, as Fenwick notes, his participation in a student-organized series of discussions about philosophical and cultural matters in his early days as a faculty member at Mount Allison. And during his year at Santa Cruz, in a similar student group, he read Spinoza, Descartes, and Kant, as he notes in a letter dated 30 January 1993. Most of his work is a model of morality, a definite — though never didactic — demonstration of both moral dilemmas and a good, that is, ethical, existence. We glean this vision of Colville as a moral philosopher from his work, but he also states his position without hesitation. ". . . I have been for many years, many decades," he writes in "A Tribute," "interested in the concept of creatures who, while living, are thinking about life. Implicit in this is the conviction that thought, and the action resulting from thought, may be good or bad." As we have seen in the context of Colville's ruminations about World War II, he does not deny the existence of evil. Compensating for our lamentable capability to inflict suffering on one another, though, he produces art that visualizes good alternatives in the philosophical sense. In fact, much of his work maintains a balance between the acknowledgement of violence, for example, in us and society, and the control of this potential. Germane are his many images of pistols (*Target Pistol and Man, Pacific, In the Woods*, and others): in each case, Colville recognizes danger but transmutes the threat into a more cerebral contemplation of life (both his and ours) and society. This transmutation doesn't completely leave the threat behind — these images affect people strongly — but it shows his thinking in action, a moral action that he sees as appropriate to art.

Colville realizes his own prescription, in "A Tribute," that "there should be a connection, delicate and difficult, between aesthetics and moral philosophy." Implicit here is that philosophy, morality, and art should act together in the public sphere, in a popular context. Colville's firm belief in the applicability of moral ideas in the world has been fundamental to many of his choices. It is a philosophical position that he has applied to the question of having his work photographically reproduced, for example, or to making relatively affordable serigraph prints for "a segment of the public which doesn't have enough money to buy paintings," as he wrote in "Some Observations." As with his affinity for literature, Colville has developed his ideas in tandem with a number of important authors. He is an independent thinker yet claims that his ideas are not especially original. For example, he has been influenced by the writings of Grant mostly because, as he writes in "A Tribute," ". . . George embodied the idea of a man thinking about how one might be good in the present and actual world. . . . Thus [he] was for me a kind of *proof.*" My "life and work have been . . . confirmed by his thought."

If we compile a list of philosophers whom Colville reads, we see a pattern. In all his philosophical inspirations — as in his art historical and literary preferences — he finds confirmation and refinements of his propensities and ideas. The most influential thinkers have been the French existentialists Sartre, Camus, Simone de Beauvoir (1908–), and especially Simone Weil (1909–43). Another important perspective has come from Hannah Arendt's (1906–) *The Human Condition* (1958), which Colville read "around 1960," he notes in the letter of 30 January 1993. He also refers to the German existentialist Martin Heidegger (1889–1976) and, as we've seen, to André Malraux. Of his contemporaries, Colville has been especially taken with the work of Grant and Murdoch. He also admires less well-known thinkers such as Jerome Bruner.

Colville mentioned Bruner's ideas in a talk at the University of Guelph in 1988. He'd read the recently published *Actual Minds, Possible Worlds* (1986), in which Bruner's challenging mix of psychology, philosophy, and literary theory results in an analysis of (among other topics) the "ways the text affects the reader," and the salient differences between what he calls a "logico-scientific" and a "narrative" mode of arranging information. Colville appreciates writers who try to understand the psychological dimensions of art, and he is keenly concerned with narrative, with both an artist's or writer's role in constructing stories and a viewer's or reader's role in receiving them. While he is preoccupied with moral themes in his work, he is not judgemental. Bruner asserts that "it is far more important, for appreciating the human condition, to understand the ways human beings construct their worlds . . . than it is to establish the ontological status of the products of these processes." In other words, he confirms what Colville knows: ontology — different realms of being, say animal and human — is significant, but more important is how we relate to, and negotiate with, the ontological differences we perceive and even construct.

Colville met Iris Murdoch and her husband, John Bayley, at a symposium organized by McMaster University and held in an Anglican retreat in Dundas, Ontario, in July 1963. The group of two dozen or so gathered there represented a range of academic disciplines and spent a week in wide-ranging discussions. There is much in Murdoch's philosophical speculations that appeals to Colville and confirms his own well-reasoned worldview. He continues to read her work. For Christmas in 1992, he received her *Metaphysics as a Guide to Morals* (1992) and found it "enormously" interesting, as he notes in a letter dated 4 June 1993. To appreciate the affinity between Colville and Murdoch, we need only return to *The Sovereignty of Good* (1971), a collection of essays in which she asserts that "To do philosophy is to explore one's own temperament, and yet at the same time to attempt to discover the truth." Certainly Colville has explored his own temperament, perhaps most directly in images of himself, such as *Target Pistol and Man, Dog and Groom*, or *Traveller*, but also in works that reflect, both visually and cerebrally, the conditions of his familial life. Murdoch is, of course, a professional philosopher and writer, just as Colville is a professional artist. Like her, he aims to see his ideas in action in the world; to George Grant he once commented approvingly, as he notes in "A Tribute," that ". . . Sartre, Camus, Simone de Beauvoir (and Iris Murdoch) had turned from philosophy to fiction in order to make ideas . . . *work*. . . ." As we've seen, communication with his audience is crucial to Colville the moral philosopher, and he tries to make his images both accessible and memorable for this reason.

Murdoch also confirms his belief in art as a force that can encourage thinking in the world. "But there can be no substitute for pure, disciplined, professional speculation," she contends, "and it is from . . . art and ethics . . . that we must hope to generate concepts worthy, and also able, to guide and check the increasing power of science." Colville is, of course, a paragon of discipline, and his rigorous conceptual and material methods of producing art ensure that he has a voice. He is not opposed to science and technology, but the values evident in his works are decidedly humanistic, ones not always represented in our lives. For Murdoch and Colville alike, then, appropriate — indeed necessary — questions for both philosopher and artist are, as she asks, "What is a good man like? How can we make ourselves morally better?"

CHOICE AND FREEDOM

She explores two other themes important to Colville: freedom of choice and its responsibilities. She ties these themes to French

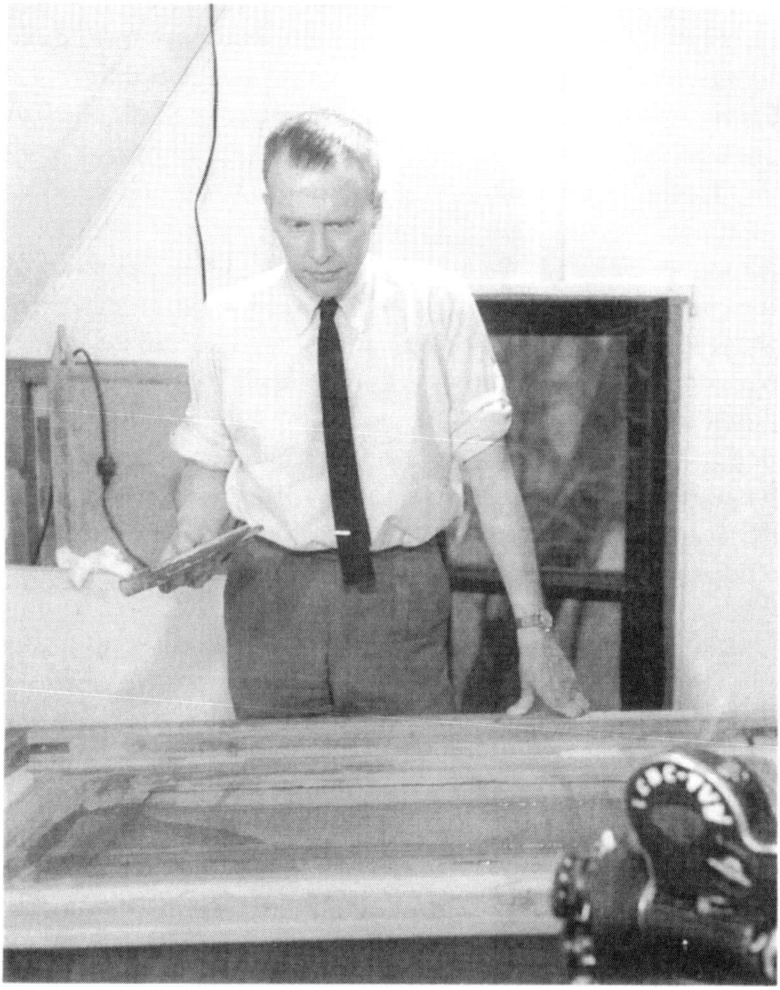

FIGURE 20

Colville printing serigraph Ravens at the Dump, *1965: CBC camera in lower right was used for first documentary about Colville,* Diary of Alex Colville *(1965).*

existentialism: "[The] return to self, that concern with the purity of the solitary will, . . . is favoured by all brands of existentialism. Here I stand alone, in total responsibility and freedom, and can only properly and responsibly do what is intelligible to me. . . ." I have stressed Colville's decisive and directed self-fashioning as an artist, and he is, on the one hand, convinced of the necessity and feasibility of making rational choices. To recall his most colloquial formulation of this view, "If you don't like Detroit, get out of Detroit." We do have the will and freedom to act in this way. On the other hand, Colville (again in concert with Murdoch) knows that fate intervenes, that we cannot always control our lives. For him — echoing Kant, I believe — "limitation is freedom," as he says in Dow's monograph. The "limitation" of an animal, he suggests in *Diary*, allows it to perform "its function more completely than any human does." If we counter that animals act mostly from instinct and are not free in a human sense, then Colville might point to his reliance on mathematical schemes in the construction of his images. Asked if he finds the "mathematical approach a limiting factor," he responds in *Diary*, "No, on the contrary it's a liberating thing. . . . [Because] the multiplicity of choices within this kind of limited mathematical scheme is enormous, . . . but they are related choices, choices within a family." It is the system, then, the set of rules, that allows us individual freedom, which, we might say, determines the context in which we must make responsible choices.

Typical of his ability to make connections, Colville further exemplifies this notion that the limitations of a system provide him with the freedom he needs with an illustration about his technical and philosophical concerns in reaching a wide audience with his work. "One of the appeals of print-making," he suggests in "Some Observations,"

> is the discipline of the printing technique; in painting almost anything is possible — in print-making there are limitations of means; the concept must be adapted to a more economical mode of expression. Print-making could even be called

> "the art of the possible," and it is interesting to observe that this art-form does have an at least tenuous connection with politics and public life — I think there is always a tendency for the print to be directed to a wider public. . . .

Colville also met George Grant at the McMaster symposium. Although they weren't "intimate" friends, as he notes in "A Tribute," they did exchange sympathetic views. Typically the painter did not simply borrow ideas from the philosopher. In Grant's work, Colville finds confirmation of his beliefs about morality in the arts and government. And in Grant himself, he found a model human with principles and a commitment to thinking and acting in the public arena. In "A Tribute," Colville provides two descriptions of Grant that tell us as much about his own ideas as about Grant's. He casts him first as an "aristocrat," a term of utmost approbation for Colville, suggesting as it does stature in society and personal authority. We've seen that Colville sees himself — though not without some self-conscious irony — as an aristocrat, and that he admired aristocratic qualities in Professor Shih when interviewing her for the directorship of the National Gallery of Canada.

Undeniably Colville is interested in class. His father was an immigrant steelworker never satisfied with his lot in Canada. His paternal grandfather, he notes in "A Tribute," was a "carter" in Scotland. His mother was a milliner before her marriage, and later ran a store that Colville remembers well. But he is also certain that one can, in effect, change class, become an aristocrat. How? Again a remark about Grant provides a clue. Speaking to the Carleton University audience about Grant after his death in 1988, Colville is careful to refer to his friend as "Professor" Grant. Clarifying his formal tone, he says, ". . . I use the title 'professor' as a form of homage. (I would like to see people who teach in universities referred to as Mr., Miss, Ms; the most significant would be called Professor)." In another and earlier context, according to notes in the Helen J. Dow Fonds, "the duty of the artist is to instruct, to give the world the moral standard it now lacks, and to make people aware of this responsibility. To be a professor means 'to profess,' to have an opinion and to broadcast it." How, then, does one move up the class ladder? Through learning and achievement, and by having a positive, moral effect in the world. By these standards, Colville has indeed become an aristocrat, a member of the international meritocracy.

Colville's passing references to Plato, Aristotle, or implicitly in "Statement" to Heidegger's focus on ontology as his own main interest demonstrate his learning and philosophical bent. When it comes to the work of André Malraux, the influence runs deeper. Colville read *The Psychology of Art* "with enormous interest" in the early 1950s, as he notes in a letter of 30 January 1993, and it's easy to understand how he absorbed Malraux's basic premise that art relies more on earlier art than on other societal forces. Malraux also champions the comparison between contemporary and earlier achievements in art that Colville practises when he sees a place for himself in art history. Colville exemplifies the benefits of Malraux's famous idea of the "Museum without walls," an "Imaginary Art Museum without precedent [that] has come into being" through photographic technology. Colville can not only compare himself with artists from ancient Egypt to the present but also think himself their equal.

Colville is as fascinated by political as by moral ideas. Both directions take him into the world. He has studied Hannah Arendt's analyses of totalitarianism, extreme abuses of power during the Nazi period (he cites as influential *Eichmann in Jerusalem* [1963]), and the necessity for some sort of response, for action. Even more impressive for him is the work of Simone Weil, especially *The Need for Roots: Prelude to a Declaration of Duties towards Mankind* (published posthumously in 1969). Weil's work was also a point of contact between Colville and Grant, both of whom were "moved," Colville notes in "A Tribute," by her life and writings.

Her life couldn't be more different from Colville's: a French Jew fascinated by Christian mysticism, and active — then injured — in the Spanish Civil War, she wrote *The Need for Roots* during

World War II in an attempt to understand France's fall to the Nazis. In despair over the Holocaust and attempting to experience the horrors wrought by the Nazis, she committed suicide by starvation in 1943. Her book reads like a guide to Colville's beliefs, even to his pictures. Much of it is structured through a listing and analysis of what she deems the soul's fundamental needs. "The first . . . ," she claims, "the one which touches most nearly [the soul's] eternal destiny, is order. . . ." This need for "order" reminds us of Colville's deepest proclivities, and Weil — like Murdoch after her — looks to art for a model of this fundamental quality:

> The contemplation of veritable works of art, and much more still that of the beauty of the world, and again much more that of the unrealized good to which we aspire, can sustain us in our efforts to think continually about that human order which should be the subject uppermost in our minds.

In the 1950s, when Colville read Weil's book, he was established as an artist yet searching for confirmation of his against-the-grain preference for rational, realist art. Then as now, "order" captures the essence of his work, an essence perceived by the producers of the first major film on Colville, entitled *Splendour of Order* and aired on CBC Television on 7 July 1985.

Another crucial need articulated by Weil is "Liberty, . . . the ability to choose," and its importance to Colville requires no further emphasis. She also claims that "obedience is a vital need of the human soul. It is of two kinds: obedience to established rules and obedience to human beings looked upon as leaders." We've seen how Colville admires — if not exactly obeys — such worthy leaders as George Grant and Robert Stanfield. Linked to obedience is the need for "Hierarchism," which "is composed of a certain veneration, a certain devotion towards superiors . . . considered . . . as symbols." Colville not only demonstrates this need but has also become a symbol of authority in Canada, an aristocrat of art. Completing Weil's list of needs are "responsi-

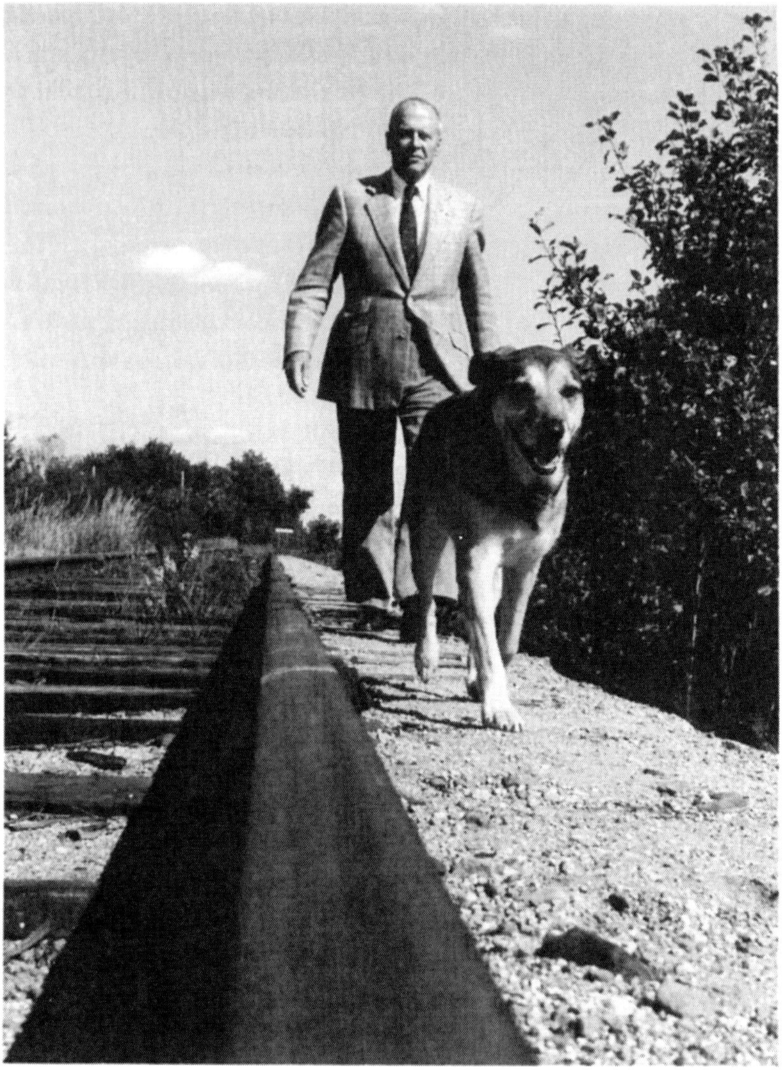

FIGURE 21

Colville with his dog Min, Wolfville, Nova Scotia, 1991.

bility" toward others and oneself, "equality" — by which she means respect for others — "security," "private property," and "truth."

The second section of *The Need for Roots* examines "uprootedness," in which these needs are impossible to satisfy, and in which individuals and societies therefore collapse. Colville fears uprootedness, and he battles it by always being in touch with what's going on in his familiar setting. Weil states that "To be rooted is perhaps the most important and least recognized need of the human soul." Colville echoes this insight. The characteristic calm of his works seeks to counteract the existential uncertainty of uprootedness. Even so, he cannot completely erase his anxiety, which is partly why many viewers notice a tension in much of his work. "Even though I'm thought of as successful," he claims in a 1991 article by Deirdre Hanna, "I never have a sense of assurance that I'm doing something well. There is always the difficult job of getting it right. It's like a kid riding a bike — 'Look Ma, no hands!' Well, I always have my hands locked to the handlebar." Colville isn't referring only to technical difficulties; as we've seen from Burnett, he still fears not having, and being able to work through, ideas.

Colville's "handlebars" are his rootedness and rigorous methods. Once again Weil's words describe him perfectly: "Everything in creation is dependent on method, including the points of intersection between this world and the next." Perhaps her point is captured in the phrase, "You make your own luck." For Colville, as for all of us, there is good and bad fortune. Method influences which sort we have in greater measure. He was lucky to come across Weil's work, but even in the 1950s reading philosophy was for him no accident.

FRENCH EXISTENTIALISM

Colville has frequently emphasized the importance of French existentialist thinking in his life, an importance, he stresses, that is now hard to understand. Even as relatively early in his career as 1965, he reports, in Dow's monograph, that "I don't think so much, at least consciously, of existentialism now, but it was really a major preoccupation of mine ten and fifteen years ago. . . ." He maintains that the writings of Sartre and Camus especially were popular, intelligible to "non-specialized" people. Their ideas thus helped him right after World War II, when he was struggling — as many of his generation did — with "the questions of conduct which were raised by the Nazi phenomenon and the holocaust," as he puts it in "A Tribute." We should remember that Colville had witnessed atrocities at the Belsen concentration camp. Partly because of his experience, he adds, "The question in my mind at the end of the war was, 'What does it mean?' There were questions of not only what to think, but of what to do."

Existentialist philosophy contends not only with manifest absurdity in our lives — the senseless violence of war, for example — but also with the necessity and responsibility of personal choice. Choice, for existentialists, defines the human state. Even though order in the world is deceptive — fragile in Colville's sense — we make our lives and the society around us by choosing our destinies. From these ideas — and Weil's version of them with respect to the rebuilding of France after World War II — Colville derived the heady feeling, as he recalls in the interview, that "when the war is over, we have a blank sheet" and can really improve society. His optimism was tempered but never extinguished. In fact, in his art and personal life in the forty or so years since he was first concerned with this philosophy, he has constructed a moral world of lasting values, in which he is sure of its principles yet cognizant of its tenuousness.

It wouldn't be appropriate to conclude too neatly a biography of Alex Colville. Although his works and habits have followed a consistent pattern for nearly forty-five years, he is a complex person who — like his work — changes and develops in subtle ways. As Burnett remarks in the interview, Colville continues to produce pictures as challenging as ever. He is anything but a closed book: events in his life, and images that he produces over the coming years, may well alter how we interpret his past. Colville reveres the past and its traditions, yet he looks toward the future and his place in it. He is concerned with the reputation that he and his work will have generations from now. In the introduction to Burnett's 1983 retrospective account of his work, Colville wrote: "Last year I was looking at Titian's *Death of Acteon* in the National Gallery in London. It is thought that he painted this affecting work in his nineties. I like to think that I may have another thirty years of work ahead of me" (15). With these words and his actions over the years, he inscribes himself prominently in art's history, its future, and in the culture of Canada.

NOTES

1 I am not the first person to have noticed the correspondence between Colville's life and art. Virgil Hammock noted the resemblance in 1976, claiming even then that it is nearly a truism among those who know Colville. I argue, however, that there is more than a resemblance, that Colville has explicitly fashioned his life after his artistic ideals.

2 *Glazed Tempera*, a dramatic version of his images, was presented by the Nightwood Theatre group at Theatre Passe Muraille. The forty-five minute production opened in June 1980. For a review, see Sharp.

3 The following is a list of works produced by Colville between the time of his retrospective exhibition in 1983 and July 1993. Works designated (s) are serigraphs; the others are acrylic paintings on particle board. In 1983: *Kingfisher* (s), *Rat* (s), *Verandah*; 1984: *Horse and Girl, Fête Champêtre* (s), *Boat and Bather*; 1985: *Bell Buoy and Cormorant* (s), *Taxi, Western Star*; 1986: *Singer, Cat and Dog, Köln Express* (s), *Low Tide*; 1987: *White Canoe, Le Chien d'or* (s), *Woman with Revolver*; 1988: *Looking Down, French Cross, Stove* (s); 1989: *Bat, Woman on Diving Board, Kiss with Honda*; 1990: *Target Shooting, Raven* (s), *Floating Woman*; 1991: *Dog and Groom, Chaplain, Arrival*; 1992: *Traveller, Couple on Bridge*; 1993; *Bridge and Raven* (s). Most of these works are to be exhibited at the Museum of Fine Arts, Montreal, in the fall of 1994.

4 For a detailed discussion of Colville's working methods, see Burnett 19–22.

5 Colville couldn't have known about Jackson's disapproval, but a later comment about this cofounder of the legendary Group of Seven serves as poetic justice. Talking about his ambitions and achievements in art, Colville claims in "The World," "I have always taken myself seriously, even as a kid. I always thought, 'I'm going to try to do really great things.' . . . I think we should go all out. So if someone were to compare me with A.Y. Jackson, I would be offended." In Johnson's article, moreover, Colville reports that "people are always asking me, 'did you admire the group of Seven?' The answer is simply no."

6 *Alex Colville: Diary of a War Artist* is a compilation of Colville's reflections about his time in the army. These reflections were recorded at disparate times: some are diary entries made on the spot, others are from interviews conducted in 1980, and a few are from interviews for the National Film Board's *Ashes of War*. I will refer to the time of his recollections when appropriate.

7 The investiture took place in 1968 because Colville was a visiting artist at the University of California, Santa Cruz, in 1967. He was on the first list of those appointed to this order.

8 For a map of the places depicted by Colville, see Burnett.

9 See Fulford, "Psychiatrist's."

10 For an equally detailed account of a more recent work, see his comments about *Traveller* (1992) in *Colville: Beings in Time.*

11 Dow dates the statement to 1964, adding that Colville said the same in 1961.

CHRONOLOGY

1920 David Alexander Colville is born on 24 August in Toronto, the second son of David and Florence Colville.

1927 The family moves to St. Catharines, Ontario.

1929 The family moves to Amherst, Nova Scotia.

1942 Colville graduates with a BFA from Mount Allison University (Sackville, NB). He enters the Canadian army and marries Rhoda Wright of Wolfville, Nova Scotia, on 5 August.

1943 He receives his commission in the army on 11 September.

1944 He goes overseas as a war artist in May. Graham is born on 15 July.

1945 Colville returns to Canada in October and continues to serve as a war artist in Ottawa.

1946 He is demobilized from the army in June and soon begins teaching at Mount Allison University. John is born on 26 July.

1948 Charles is born on 15 February.

1949 Ann is born on 6 August.

1951 Colville has his first solo exhibition, at the New Brunswick Museum in Saint John.

1953 He has his first solo exhibition in the United States, at the Hewitt Gallery in New York.

1955 He has his second solo exhibition at the Hewitt Gallery.

1958 He exhibits at the Hart House Gallery (the University of Toronto) and Laing Galleries in Toronto.

1963 Colville receives the Dunn International Award from the Beaverbrook Art Gallery in Fredericton and exhibits at the Banfer Gallery in New York.

He resigns from teaching at Mount Allison University.

1965 He is commissioned to design Canada's centennial coins.

1966 He represents Canada at the XXXIII Venice Biennale Exhibition. The National Gallery of Canada purchases *To Prince Edward Island.*

1967 Colville becomes an Officer of the Order of Canada and receives an honorary degree (D.Litt.) from Trent University (Peterborough).

1967–68 He is a visiting artist at the University of California (Santa Cruz).

1968 He receives an honorary degree (LLD) from Mount Allison University.

1969 Colville exhibits at Kestner-Gesellschaft in Hannover, Germany, and he receives an honorary degree (LLD) from Dalhousie University (Halifax).

1970 He exhibits at the Marlborough Fine Art Gallery in London, England.

1971 He is a visiting artist in West Berlin.

1973 Colville moves to his present home in Wolfville and receives honorary degrees (LLD) from Simon Fraser University (Burnaby) and the University of Windsor.

1975 He receives the Molson Prize (Canada Council) and an honorary degree (D.Litt.) from Acadia University (Wolfville).

1976 He exhibits at the Norman Mackenzie Art Gallery in Regina. His brother Robert, born in 1915, dies.

1977 He exhibits at Gemeentmuseum in Arnhem, Netherlands; Kunsthalle in Düsseldorf, West Germany; and Fischer Fine Art in London, England.

1978 Colville designs a medal for Governor General and Mrs. Jules Léger and exhibits at the Mira Godard Gallery in Toronto and Montreal.

1981 He is appointed chancellor of Acadia University, becomes the Brockington Lecturer at Queen's University (Kingston), and receives an honorary degree (D.Litt.) from Memorial University (St. John's).

1982 He becomes a Companion of the Order of Canada.

1983–84 Colville's retrospective exhibition travels to six Canadian and German galleries.

1984–85 He exhibits in Beijing, Hong Kong, Tokyo, and London, England.

1987 The Colvilles acquire the dog Min.

1988 Their dog Dinah dies.

1990 Colville receives an honorary degree (LLD) from the University of Calgary and becomes a board member of the National Gallery of Canada (to 1993).

1991 He exhibits at The Drabinsky Gallery in Toronto and resigns as chancellor of Acadia University.

1992 The Colvilles acquire the cat Tideways, and Colville is appointed to the Privy Council.

1993 An exhibition of Colville's drawings, travelling to six Canadian galleries, begins (1993–95).

WORKS CONSULTED

Baele, Nancy. "Alex Colville: The Artist as Autobiographer." *Citizen* [Ottawa] 23 July 1983: 27.

Boyd, Margaret. "Art Appreciation Mystery to Colville." *Daily Mercury* [Guelph] 19 Mar. 1988: 15.

Bruce, Harry. "Death, Art and Alex Colville: A Unique Menace Behind Those Canvases." *Saturday Night* May 1972: 30–34.

Bruner, Jerome. *Actual Minds, Possible Worlds.* Cambridge: Harvard UP, 1986.

Burnett, David. *Colville.* Toronto: Art Gallery of Ontario; McClelland, 1983.

______. Personal Interview. 17 Dec. 1992.

Cheetham, Mark A. "The World, the Work, and the Artist: Colville and the Communality of Vision." *RACAR* 15.1 (1988): 58–63.

Colville, Alex. Address. Public Affairs Assembly. University of Toronto Schools. Toronto, 22 Oct. 1992.

______. "Alex Colville on Alex Colville." *Alex Colville: Diary of a War Artist.* Comp. Graham Metson and Cheryl Lean. Halifax: Nimbus, 1981. 21–23.

______. "Alex Colville on His Centennial Coins." Dow, *The Art of Alex Colville*, 208–09.

______. Interview. *Stereo Morning.* CBC Radio, 12 Aug. 1992.

______. Letter to the author. 9 Sept. 1987.

______. Letter to the author. 15 Jan. 1992.

______. Letter to the author. 4 June 1992.

______. Letter to the author. 9 Dec. 1992.

______. Letter to the author. 30 Jan. 1993.

______. "My Experience as a Painter and Some General Views of Art." Dow, *The Art of Alex Colville*, 203–08.

______. Personal interview. 9 Nov. 1992.

______. "Some Observations on My Serigraphs." Unpublished essay, 1976.

______ . "Statement." Dow, *The Art of Alex Colville*, 209–10.
______ . "A Tribute to Professor George P. Grant." The Legacy of *Lament for a Nation*. Bell Lecture Series. Carleton U, Ottawa, Sept. 1989.
______ . "War Diary and Other Recollections." *Alex Colville: Diary of a War Artist*. Comp. Graham Metson and Cheryl Lean. Halifax: Nimbus, 1981. 25–159.
Colville: Beings in Time [exhibition catalogue]. North Bay, ON: W.K.P. Kennedy Gallery, 1992.
Diary of Alex Colville. With Ken Homer. Prod. Sally Lumsden. 20/20. CBC Television. 6 June 1965.
Dow, Helen J. *The Art of Alex Colville*. Toronto: McGraw, 1972.
______ . Helen J. Dow Fonds. Edward P. Taylor Research Library, Art Gallery of Ontario, Toronto.
Eliot, T.S. "Tradition and the Individual Talent." *Selected Prose of T.S. Eliot*. Ed. Frank Kermode. London: Faber, 1975. 37–44.
Eakin, Paul John. *Fictions in Autobiography: Studies in the Art of Self-Invention*. Princeton: Princeton UP, 1985.
Fenwick, Roly. Telephone interview. 21 Oct. 1992.
Fulford, Robert. "Painter Laureate." *Saturday Night* July 1983: 5–6.
______ . "A Psychiatrist's Odyssey." *Saturday Night* Feb. 1984: 34+.
Godard, Mira. Personal interview. 14 Oct. 1992.
______ . Personal interview. 15 Dec. 1992.
Hammock, Virgil G. "Alex Colville: Perfection and Reality." *Vie des arts* 21 (1976): 86–89.
Hanna, Deirdre. "Success Can't Stay Colville's Anxieties." *Now* [Toronto] 24–30 Oct. 1991: 63.
Johnson, Eve. "Images out of the Ordinary." *Vancouver Sun* 14 June 1984: B1.
Malraux, André. *The Psychology of Art*. Trans. Stuart Gilbert. 3 vols. New York: Pantheon, 1949–50.
Mays, John Bentley. "Colville's Importance Exaggerated." *Globe and Mail* [Toronto] 23 July 1983: E13.
______ . " 'I Value Most My Absolute Freedom': Alex Colville Loves Small-Town Life, Ideally Thousands of Miles Away from Other Artists." *Globe and Mail* [Toronto] 23 July 1983: E1.
Murdoch, Iris. *The Sovereignty of Good*. New York: Schocken, 1971.
Nakoneshny, Shane D. "Alex Colville." *ArtsAtlantic* 43 (1992): 11–12.

Ohff, Heinz. "Provinziell wie Caspar David Friedrich." *Der Tagesspiegel* [Berlin] 25 Aug. 1971: 4.

Perry, Richard A. "Alex Colville: Why Have We Made Him Head Boy of Canadian Painters?" *Canadian Forum* Mar. 1985: 6–12.

Reid, Dennis. *A Concise History of Canadian Painting*. 2nd ed. Toronto: Oxford UP, 1988.

Sharp, Debra. "Bid to Dramatize Colville Works." *Globe and Mail* [Toronto] 21 June 1980: 8.

Stewart, Walter P. "Alex Colville, Realist Painter." *Atlantic Advocate* 3 Nov. 1976: 9–12.

"The Sweetest Spring." Writ. and dir. Eric Till. *Adrienne Clarkson Presents*. CBC Television. 8 Nov. 1990.

Toupin, Gilles. "Colville, peintre de la vie moderne." *La Presse* [Montréal] 28 Oct. 1978: D22.

Weil, Simone. *The Need for Roots: Prelude to a Declaration of Duties towards Mankind*. Trans. A.F. Wills. London: Routledge, 1952.

Werner, Hans. "Nothing Phoney." *Canadian Art* 4.3 (1987): 70–76.

Young-Bruel, Elisabeth. *Creative Characters*. New York: Routledge, 1991.